WordPerfect
Made Simple

Made Simple *Computer Books*

- easy to follow
- jargon free
- practical
- task based
- easy steps

All you want are the basics, you don't want to be bothered with all the advanced stuff, or be engulfed in technical mumbo jumbo — you have neither the time not the interest in knowing about every feature, function or command and you don't want to wade through big computer books on the subject or stumble through the maze of information in the manuals... then the

MADE SIMPLE series is for you!

You want to learn quickly what's essential and how to do things with a particular piece of software... you're :

- a Secretary, or temp for example... who wants to get the job done, quickly and efficiently

- a Manager, without the time to learn all about the software but who wants or needs to produce letters, memos, reports, spreadsheets for example

- a person working from home using the software, who needs a self teaching approach, that gives results fast, with the least confusion.

By a combination of tutorial approach, with tasks to do, and easy steps the MADE SIMPLE series of Computer Books stands above all others.

See the complete series at your local bookstore now, or in case of difficulty, contact Reed Book Services Ltd, Orders Dept, PO Box 5, Rushden, Northants, NN10 9YX. Tel: 0933 58521. Fax: 0933 50284. Credit card sales: 0933 410511

Series titles:

AmiPro	Moira Stephen	0 7506 2067 6
Excel	Stephen Morris	0 7506 2070 6
Lotus 1-2-3	Ian Robertson	0 7506 2066 8
MS-Dos	Ian Sinclair	0 7506 2069 2
MS-Works	P. K. McBride	0 7506 2065 X
Windows	P. K. McBride	0 7506 2072 2
Word	Keith Brindley	0 7506 2071 4
WordPerfect	Stephen Copestake	0 7506 2068 4

WordPerfect
Made Simple

Stephen Copestake

MADE SIMPLE
BOOKS

Made Simple
An imprint of Butterworth-Heinemann Ltd
Linacre House, Jordan Hill, Oxford OX2 8DP

ℛ A member of the Reed Elsevier group

OXFORD   LONDON   BOSTON
MUNICH   NEW DELHI   SINGAPORE   SYDNEY
TOKYO   TORONTO   WELLINGTON

First published 1994

British Library Cataloguing in Publication Data
A catalogue record for this book is available from the British
Library

ISBN 0 7506 2068 4

Typeset and produced by Co-publications, Loughborough
Set in Archetype, Cotswold Book and Gravity from Advanced
Graphics Limited
Icons designed by Sarah Ward © 1994
Printed and bound in Great Britain
by Scotprint, Musselburgh, Scotland

Contents

Preface

The computer is about as simple as a spacecraft, and who ever let an untrained spaceman loose? You pick up a manual that weighs more than your birth-weight, open it and find it's written in computerspeak. You see messages on the screen resembling some strange spy code and the thing even makes noises. No wonder you feel it's your lucky day if everything goes right. What do you do if everything goes wrong? Give up.

Training helps. Being able to type helps. Experience helps. This book helps, by providing training and assisting with experience. It can't help you if you always manage to hit the wrong keys, but it *can* tell you which are the right ones and what to do when you hit the wrong ones. After some time, even the dreaded manual will start to make sense, just because you at last know what the writers are wittering on about.

Computing is not black magic. You don't need luck or charms, just a bit of understanding. The problem is that the programs used nowadays *look* simple — but simply aren't. Most are crammed with features you don't need — but how do you know what you don't need? This book shows you what is essential and guides you through it. You will know how to make an action work and why. Less essential bits can wait — and once you start to use a program with confidence you can tackle those bits for yourself.

The writers of this series have all been through it. We know time is valuable, and you don't want to waste yours. You don't buy books on computer topics to read jokes or be told you are a dummy. You want to find what you need — and be shown how to do it. Here, at last, you can.

Introduction

WordPerfect 6.0 for DOS incorporates a wealth of new features/enhancements.

Here is a brief list:

● Graphics and Page modes — these display documents on screen as they will appear when printed

● document statistics — WordPerfect now supplies, as well as a word count, a series of related statistics e.g. average word length, average sentence length

● button bars — button bars are rows of on-screen icons which give immediate access to commonly used WordPerfect features and commands

● ribbon — provides on-screen access to certain very frequently used features e.g. you can pull down a list of installed typefaces without having to go into the Font menu

● File Manager — you can now manage your files and directories from within WordPerfect

● document windows — you can now have up to nine documents open at once, and these can be displayed in resizable screen windows

● scroll bars — vertical and horizontal scroll bars permit rapid movement through documents with just a mouse click

● New and Open — you can now open new documents with one command. Open now lets you open existing documents without having to close any first.

WordPerfect 6.0 for DOS also provides Text mode. This corresponds with the editing screens of earlier versions, although it has greater functionality. Use Text mode:

● if you lack an EGA, VGA or higher display, or
● for increased editing/scrolling speed.

WordPerfect Corporation has ensured that, although the number of available mouse-driven operations is reduced in Text mode (for instance, you can only scale graphics boxes in Text mode with the use of the keyboard), all keystroke combinations are identical whether you use Text, Graphics or Page modes.

Hardware requirements

The following are necessary for the correct running of WordPerfect 6.0 for DOS:

● an absolute minimum of 480 kilobytes of internal memory. 520 K is recommended. More is even better
● an 80286 chip as an absolute minimum
● MS–DOS version 3.0 or higher
● a CGA monitor in order to use Text mode
● an EGA, VGA or SVGA monitor to use Graphics and Page modes
● one high–density floppy drive
● 7–16 megabytes of available hard disk space (depending on the extent of installation).

It isn't necessary to have a mouse as virtually all WordPerfect 6's functions can be achieved through a keyboard. There are a few exceptions to this, but they're not crucial. However, using a mouse does make the program even easier to operate.

The more RAM you can free up for WordPerfect 6.0 for DOS, the better. The speed with which the program functions (this is especially true for printing) is directly related (perhaps even logarithmically) to the amount of available memory. This means that WordPerfect will run better if you have a memory manager installed on your system. Available candidates are:

● MEMMAKER — supplied with version 6.* of DOS
● QEMM
● 386 MAX

Speed improvements with the correct memory management settings can be very noticeable. However, care is essential. For instance, version 7 of 386 MAX provides DOSMAX. This lets you run DOS sessions under Microsoft Windows with much more available memory per session. There is, however, a drawback: it will only run WordPerfect 6.0 for DOS in Text (not in Graphics or Page) mode...

1　Help

Using the Help index

WordPerfect 6's Help index provides access to a large directory of very specific Help topics. Use this when you need assistance with a specific task — or one aspect of a task — which you're *not* currently engaged on (for help with current tasks, see page 9 — *Using context-sensitive Help)*

WordPerfect's Help index is organised alphabetically. You can:

● search for topics dynamically

● use the Index as a springboard to jump to other Help features.

When you search for topics, WordPerfect 6 uses *Hypertext* links to provide the information. This simply means that when you enter partial details of the topic name, WordPerfect attempts to guess the rest (and usually succeeds).

Each topic selected within the Index provides links to associated topics.

1 Choose **Help→Index**. This calls up the Help Index dialog box

2 Click Name Search

3 Begin to enter the name of the topic on which you require assistance. WordPerfect jumps to the nearest topic

4 When the correct topic is highlighted, double–click on it or choose Look

5 If you need help with an associated task, press [Home], [Home] to move to the end of the current Help task. Then double–click on the appropriate task. Or highlight it and choose Look

6 To leave Help, press [Esc] or choose Cancel

Tip:

The keyboard route to the Help index is as follows:

[F1]; Index; [Enter]

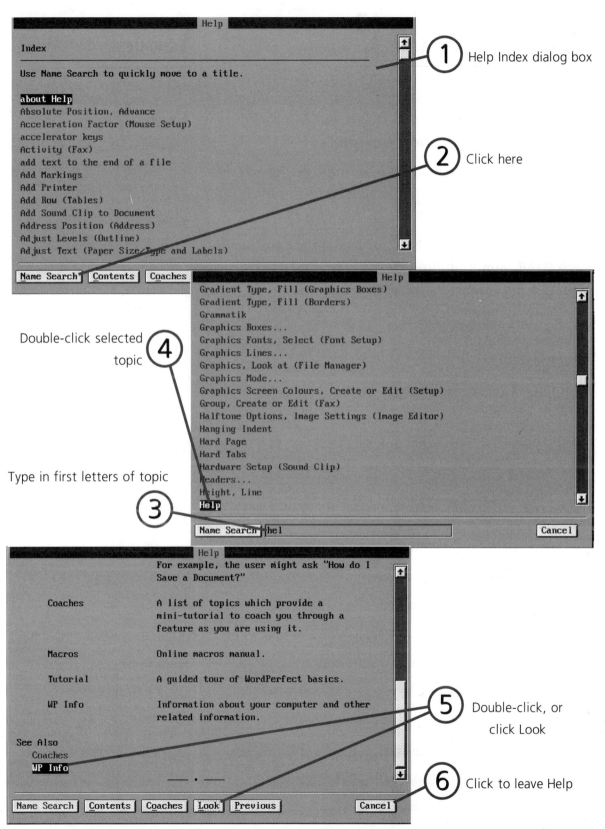

① Help Index dialog box

② Click here

Double-click selected topic ④

Type in first letters of topic ③

⑤ Double-click, or click Look

⑥ Click to leave Help

3

Using How do I?

Use How Do I? to get assistance with specific, fairly broad tasks. How Do I? provides a list of procedures which answer the question: How do I?

For instance, if you need help with adjusting tab settings, changing font settings or inserting graphic boxes (or a host of additional topics), use How Do I?

You can even use How do I? for assistance with using Help itself. Simply follow step 1. The first task – Use Help – is automatically highlighted. Now press ⏎ for help with using Help.

The Name Search feature is unavailable from within How Do I?

1 Choose **Help→How Do I**. This calls up the Help dialog box, allowing you to choose a procedure you want help with

2 Use the cursor keys and/or the Page Up and Page Down keys to scroll to the relevant task. Double–click on it, or highlight it and choose Look

3 If you need help with an associated task, press Home, Home to move to the end of the current Help task

4 Double–click on the appropriate task. Or highlight it and choose Look

5 To leave Help, press Esc or choose Cancel

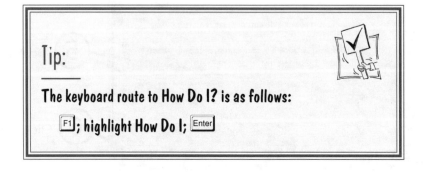

Tip:

The keyboard route to How Do I? is as follows:
F1; highlight How Do I; Enter

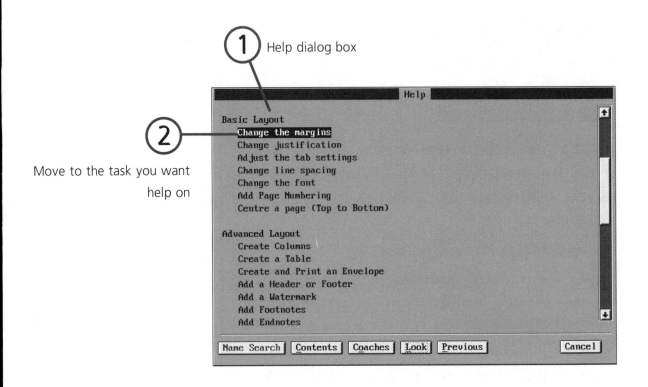

(1) Help dialog box

(2) Move to the task you want help on

(3) Press ⌂ to move to end of current Help task

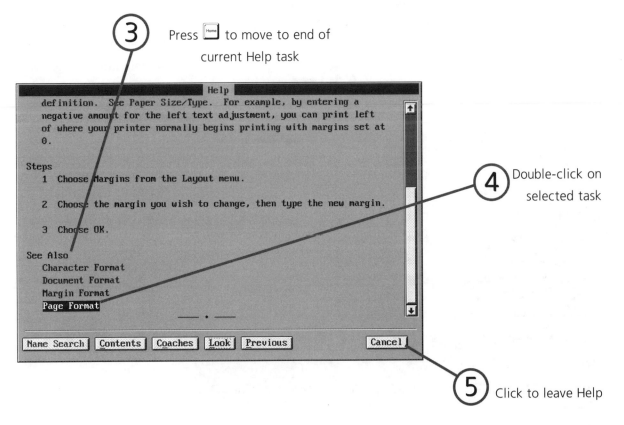

(4) Double-click on selected task

(5) Click to leave Help

Using Glossary

The WordPerfect 6 Help Glossary is a handy list of individual definitions.

There are two ways to use Glossary.

● you can click on any underlined entries within Help topics; WordPerfect then jumps to the appropriate definition

● you can access Glossary directly.

Either way, Glossary provides potted definitions of terms used throughout WordPerfect. Use Glossary as a source of clarification of specific terms rather than topics.

Example: the Glossary definition of the term click is:

> Quickly press and release the left mouse button. Alternatively, use the right mouse button if you are using a left–handed mouse.

To access Glossary from within Help topics —

1 Choose **Help↳Index** to call up the Help screen

2 Double–click the relevant topic (or highlight it and choose Look)

3 Within the topic, double-click the underlined word whose definition you need

To access Glossary directly —

4 From within the standard WordPerfect editing screen, choose **Help↳Contents** to call the Help Contents screen

5 Double–click Glossary

Help screen

```
                          Help
Adjust Text (Paper Size/Type and Labels)
Adjustment, Leading
Advance Hardware Port Setup (Printer)
Advance...
align text on the margins
ALL OTHERS (Paper Size/Type)
Allow Box to Move Page to Page with Text (Graphics Boxes)
Allow Box to Overlap Paragraph Boxes (Graphics Boxes)
Allow Box to Overlap Other Boxes (Graphics Boxes)
Allow Undo (Setup)
Amount of Footnote to Keep Together
Appearance (Font)
Append...
ASCII character set (Code Page)
Assign Variable (Macro)
Attach To (Graphics Boxes)
Attributes...
Auto Code Placement...

 Name Search    Contents    Coaches    Look    Previous          Cancel
```

Double-click the topic you want help on

6

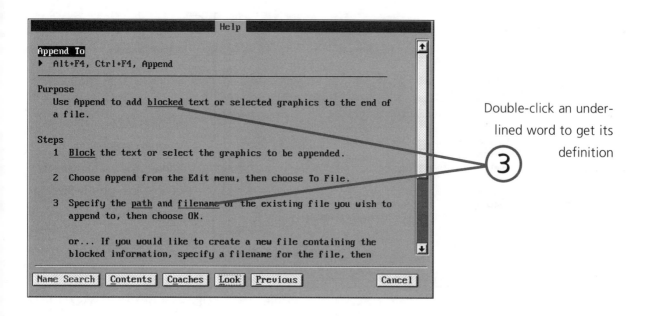

Double-click an under-
lined word to get its
definition

③

④ Help Contents screen

Double-click ⑤

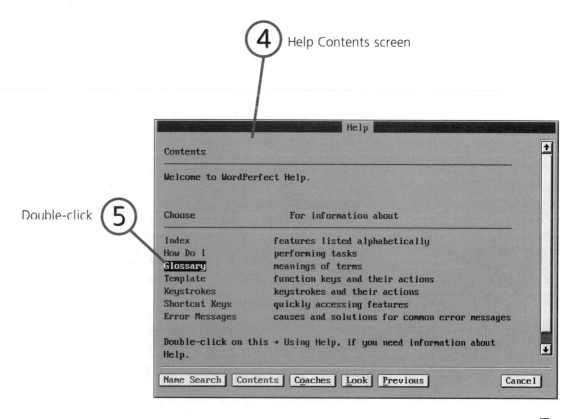

Using Glossary (contd)

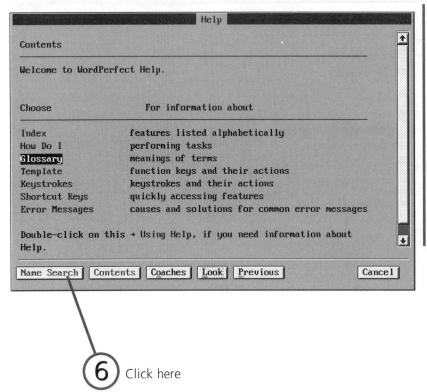

Click here

6 Within Glossary, choose
Name Search

7 Begin to enter the term
whose definition you
require. When
WordPerfect has high-
lighted the correct term,
double–click on it (or
choose Look)

Tip:

The keyboard route to Glossary is:

⌨ F1 ; **Glossary**

Enter the first few letters
of the task you want a
glossary of

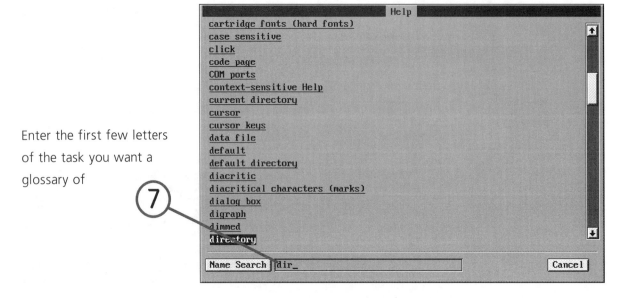

Context-sensitive Help

WordPerfect provides assistance which is directly related to the task in hand.

Use context-sensitive Help as a very useful shortcut to getting the assistance you need.

If you've just pulled down a WordPerfect menu, for example, context-sensitive Help provides assistance relating to whichever menu topic is highlighted. If you've pressed ⏎ (or Enter) over a menu topic, thereby invoking the relevant dialog box, context-sensitive Help produces a screen which relates directly to this dialog box. And so on.

In this way, you can always be sure of receiving relevant assistance.

Basic steps:

1 While engaged in the task with which you need assistance, Press F1

2 To return to the task when you've finished with context-sensitive Help, choose Cancel (or press Esc).

Take note:

The only route to context-sensitive Help is via the keyboard

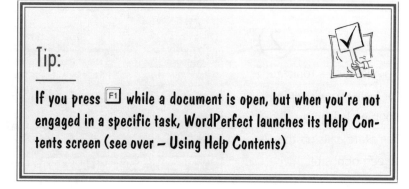

Tip:

If you press F1 while a document is open, but when you're not engaged in a specific task, WordPerfect launches its Help Contents screen (see over – Using Help Contents)

Using Help Contents

Use the Help Contents screen for access to a variety of additional, broad Help areas.

We've already covered the Index, How Do I? and Glossary options in earlier tasks. Further options in the Contents screen are:

● Template — a 'template' of function key combinations e.g. Ctrl + F2 to invoke WordPerfect's Speller (Spell Checker)

● Keystrokes — a list of special keys and their effects e.g. Page Down to move to the next page

● Shortcut keys — a list of keyboard shortcuts e.g. Ctrl + Z to undo errors

● Error Messages — a list of error messages and associated explanations.

1 Choose **Help↳Contents**. to call up the Help Contents screen

2 Double–click the topic on which you require assistance (or highlight it and choose Look)

3 If required, double–click a listed topic for additional help

4 Choose Cancel when done

(1) Help Contents screen

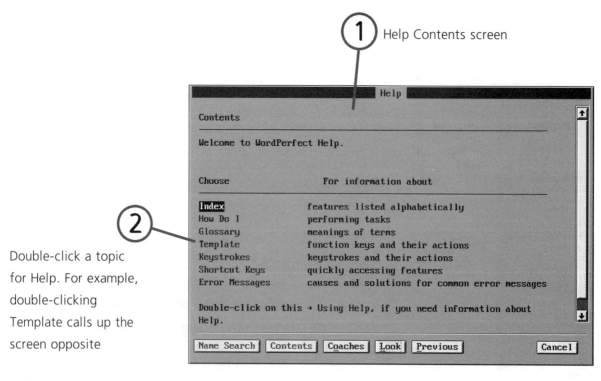

Double-click a topic for Help. For example, double-clicking Template calls up the screen opposite

```
                                        Help
 Contents                                                              ↑

 Welcome to WordPerfect Help.


 Choose                    For information about

 Index              features listed alphabetically
 How Do I           performing tasks
 Glossary           meanings of terms
 Template           function keys and their actions
 Keystrokes         keystrokes and their actions
 Shortcut Keys      quickly accessing features
 Error Messages     causes and solutions for common error messages

 Double-click on this → Using Help, if you need information about
 Help.                                                                 ↓

 Name Search   Contents   Coaches   Look   Previous            Cancel
```

③ Double-click a topic for
further help

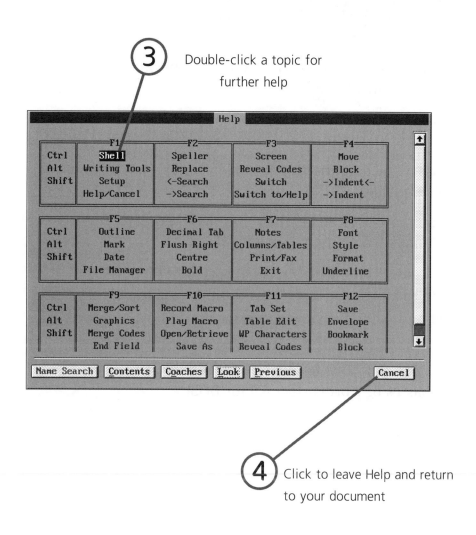

④ Click to leave Help and return
to your document

Tip:

The keyboard route to the
Help Contents screen is:

F1

Summary for Section 1

● Use the Help Index to find assistance on specific topics you can easily identify.

● Use How Do I? for assistance with overall broad topics.

● Use Glossary for definitions of common terms (arranged alphabetically).

● Use context-sensitive Help when you need assistance in the midst of performing a task.

● Use Help Contents for access to an overview of Help features, and to a variety of specialist options (e.g. for information on function keys and keystroke combinations).

● Above all, use this book for specific, accessible advice on the basics of WordPerfect 6.0 for DOS!

2   General features

Working in Text mode

WordPerfect 6 provides three screen modes: Text, Graphics and Page.

Text mode has certain advantages:

● screen drawing is much quicker, particularly on slow systems

● it works with CGA (as well as EGA and VGA) monitors.

There are also drawbacks:

● it only displays text (graphic images show up as cryptic boxes)

● you can't scale graphic images with the use of the mouse

● it makes no attempt to show your document as it will look when printed. This means, among other things, that fonts can often display misleadingly.

Basic steps:

1 Choose **View➔Text Mode**. The display changes to Text mode

2 Begin entering text

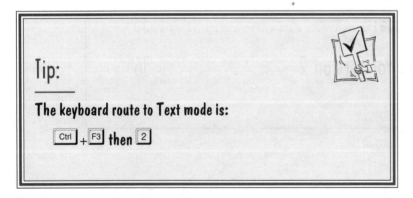

Tip:

The keyboard route to Text mode is:
`Ctrl` + `F3` then `2`

① WordPerfect's Text mode

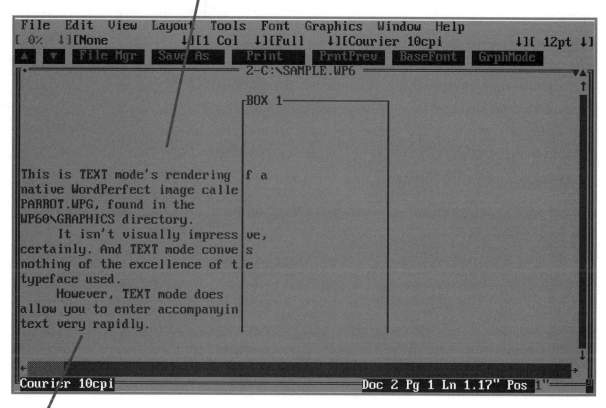

```
  File   Edit   View   Layout   Tools   Font   Graphics   Window   Help
[ 0%  ↓][None            ↓][1 Col  ↓][Full    ↓][Courier 10cpi          ↓][ 12pt ↓]
 ▲   ▼   File Mgr   Save As      Print      PrntPrev   BaseFont   GrphMode
                            2-C:\SAMPLE.WP6                            ▼▲
                                                                       ↑
                        ┌BOX 1──────────────────────┐
                        │                            │
                        │                            │
This is TEXT mode's rendering │f a                   │
native WordPerfect image calle│                      │
PARROT.WPG, found in the      │                      │
WP60\GRAPHICS directory.      │                      │
      It isn't visually impress│ve,                  │
certainly. And TEXT mode conve│s                     │
nothing of the excellence of t│e                     │
typeface used.                │                      │
      However, TEXT mode does │                      │
allow you to enter accompanyin│                      │
text very rapidly.            └──────────────────────┘
                                                                       ↓
 ←                                                                →
Courier 10cpi                          Doc 2 Pg 1 Ln 1.17" Pos 1"
```

② You can begin entering text
immediately

Tip:

Here's a suggestion. Use Text mode for preliminary work on complex documents. Then switch to Graphics or Page modes (see over) for final proofing

Graphics and Page modes

WordPerfect 6's Graphics and Page modes have a lot in common.

They both provide an excellent on–screen representation of what a document will look like when printed. This means that fonts which display on–screen will normally match printed fonts. And graphic images display faithfully; you can move and re–scale them with the use of the mouse.

Disadvantages? Yes, there are a few.

● even with a fast computer, Graphics and Page modes can sometimes be slow in updating screen displays

● you can't use them if you have a CGA (colour graphics adapter) monitor

● you need at least 520K of basic memory (550K is better).

The difference between Graphics and Page modes is that Page mode goes one step further: apart from accurately displaying the body of the document you're working on, it also shows additional components e.g. headers and footers (see page 108).

1 Choose either
View ↳Graphics Mode
or **View ↳Page Mode**

2 Edit the document normally

① WordPerfect's Graphics mode

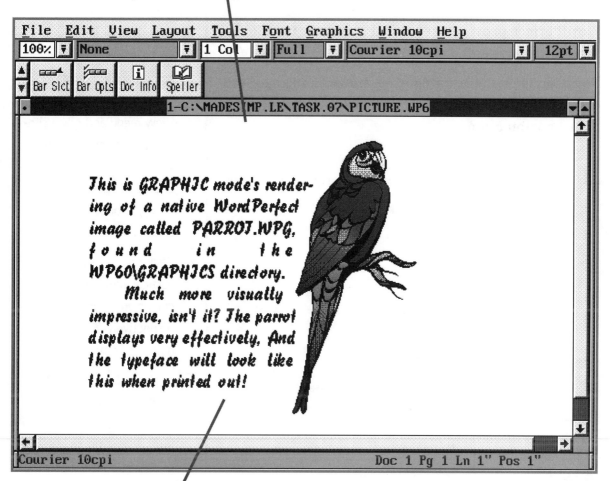

This is GRAPHIC mode's rendering of a native WordPerfect image called PARROT.WPG, found in the WP60\GRAPHICS directory.
    Much more visually impressive, isn't it? The parrot displays very effectively. And the typeface will look like this when printed out!

② This is the Graphics mode equivalent of the Text mode screen on page 15

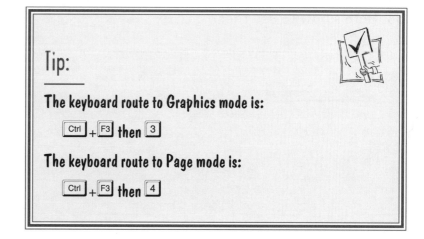

Tip:

The keyboard route to Graphics mode is:

    Ctrl + F3 then 3

The keyboard route to Page mode is:

    Ctrl + F3 then 4

17

Moving around the screen

WordPerfect provides several techniques for moving around the screen.

These divide into two categories: mouse- and keyboard-driven. The following is a list of the most useful keyboard combinations:

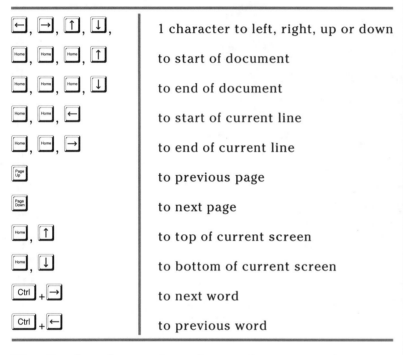

←, →, ↑, ↓,	1 character to left, right, up or down
Home, Home, Home, ↑	to start of document
Home, Home, Home, ↓	to end of document
Home, Home, ←	to start of current line
Home, Home, →	to end of current line
Page Up	to previous page
Page Down	to next page
Home, ↑	to top of current screen
Home, ↓	to bottom of current screen
Ctrl + →	to next word
Ctrl + ←	to previous word

WordPerfect 6 provides advanced mouse techniques, too. Here's how to use them.

1 First, ensure that the vertical and horizontal scroll bars are displayed. To do this, pull down the View menu and make sure Horizontal Scroll Bar and Vertical Scroll Bar are checked (that is — ticked). If not, choose them to check them

2 Click on ↑ or ↓ in the vertical scroll bar to move cursor up or down one line respectively. Click and hold for continuous scroll

3 Click on ← or → in the horizontal scroll bar to move one character to the left and right respectively. Click and hold for continuous scrolling

4 Click above or below the scroll box in either scroll bar to move the cursor one screen in the required direction. Click and hold for continuous scroll

5 Drag either scroll box along the scroll bar to move to the appropriate location in a document

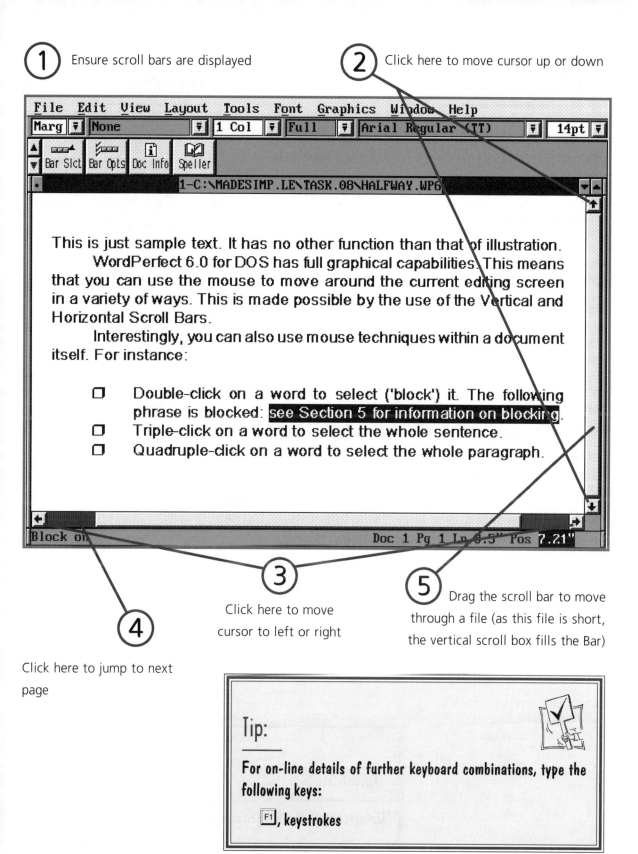

① Ensure scroll bars are displayed

② Click here to move cursor up or down

File   Edit   View   Layout   Tools   Font   Graphics   Window   Help

Marg ⊽ None   ⊽ 1 Col ⊽ Full ⊽ Arial Regular (TT)   ⊽ 14pt ⊽

Bar Slct Bar Opts Doc Info Speller

1-C:\MADESIMP.LE\TASK.08\HALFWAY.WP6

This is just sample text. It has no other function than that of illustration.
     WordPerfect 6.0 for DOS has full graphical capabilities. This means
that you can use the mouse to move around the current editing screen
in a variety of ways. This is made possible by the use of the Vertical and
Horizontal Scroll Bars.
     Interestingly, you can also use mouse techniques within a document
itself. For instance:

❑   Double-click on a word to select ('block') it. The following
       phrase is blocked: see Section 5 for information on blocking.
❑   Triple-click on a word to select the whole sentence.
❑   Quadruple-click on a word to select the whole paragraph.

Block on   Doc 1 Pg 1 Ln 3.5" Pos 7.21"

③ Click here to move
cursor to left or right

④

⑤ Drag the scroll bar to move
through a file (as this file is short,
the vertical scroll box fills the Bar)

Click here to jump to next
page

Tip:

For on-line details of further keyboard combinations, type the
following keys:

F1, keystrokes

The Ribbon

WordPerfect 6's Ribbon provides easy, on-the-spot access to various display and formatting options.

You can use it to apply:

- zoom levels
- styles
- text columns
- text justification
- typefaces
- type sizes.

For more information on these topics, see later in this book.

Using the ribbon is much simpler than pulling down a series of menus. For instance, to *right-justify* text (i.e. force it to align with the right page margin), you would first block it (see page 70). Then, using WordPerfect's menu structure, you would normally have to pull down the Layout menu, choose Line, then select Right in the Justification section of the Line Format dialog box.

It's much easier simply to click on the Justification section of the Ribbon and double-click on Right.

Basic steps:

1 First, pull down the View menu and ensure that Ribbon is checked (that is — ticked). If it isn't, the Ribbon won't display. Choose it to check it

2 Click ⬇ next to the feature you want to invoke

3 From the drop-down list of available options, double-click on the correct one

---

Take note:

Unfortunately, the Ribbon can only be used if you have a mouse.

The Ribbon. Ensure it is displayed

Click to launch feature

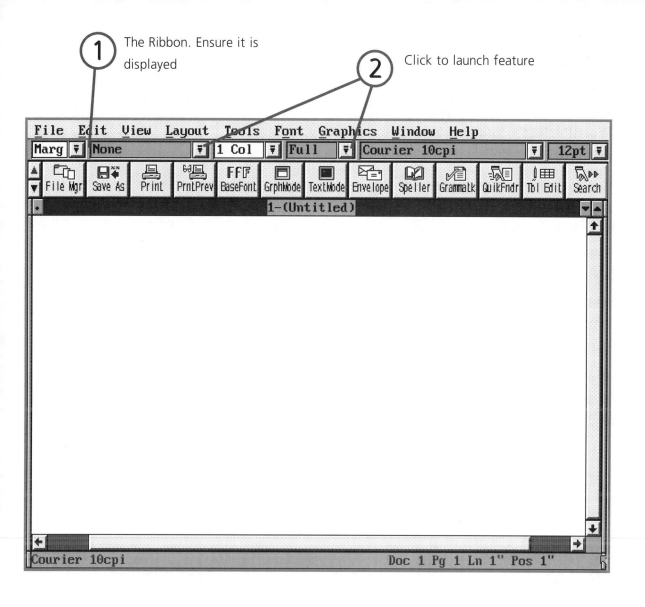

Select the option you want from the drop-down list

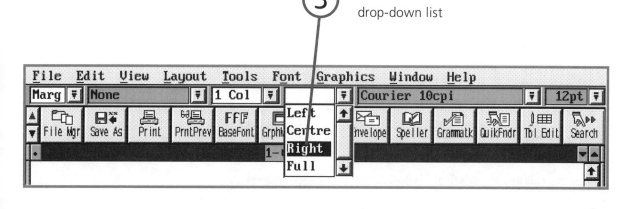

Button bars

WordPerfect's *button bars* provide easy access to commonly used commands and features.

Button bars contain *icons* — graphical representations of WordPerfect commands. By clicking on the icons, you can launch features immediately. This is often much more convenient than using WordPerfect's menu structure.

Button bars can be displayed on the screen either horizontally or vertically. You can also specify whether they should contain:

- text only
- pictures only, or
- text and pictures.

Basic steps:

1 First, pull down the View menu and make sure Button Bar is ticked. If it is, press ⎋ twice to close the menu. If it isn't ticked, choose it

2 Now click once on the appropriate icon to launch the associated feature

3 To access further icons, click ▲ or ▼ (found at the left of horizontal button bars and on the top of vertical button bars)

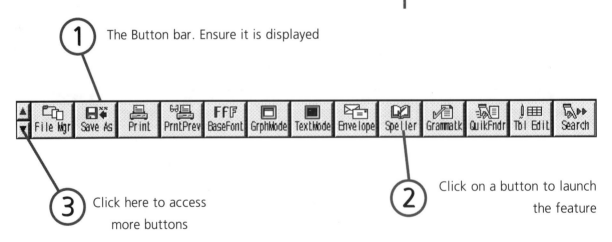

① The Button bar. Ensure it is displayed

③ Click here to access more buttons

② Click on a button to launch the feature

Take note:

You can only use WordPerfect 6's button bars if you have a mouse

4 Choose **View⤷Button Bar Setup⤷Options**.
This calls up the Button Bar Options dialog box. Make appropriate selections

5 Click OK when done

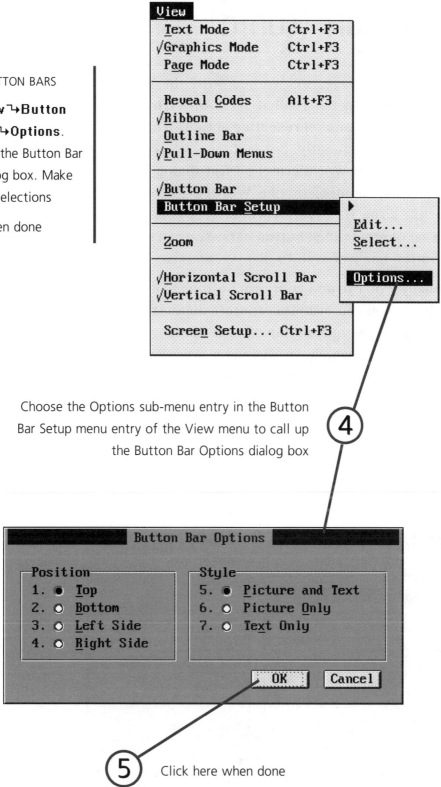

Choose the Options sub-menu entry in the Button Bar Setup menu entry of the View menu to call up the Button Bar Options dialog box

④

⑤ Click here when done

Button bars (contd)

On the previous page, we worked with the default WordPerfect button bar (called *WPMAIN*). This contains a variety of icons representing actions which are performed very frequently. For instance, you can use WPMAIN to access WordPerfect's Print dialog boxes, change display modes, invoke WordPerfect's Spell Checker and so on. However, WordPerfect 6 comes with a whole set of pre-defined button bars. You can choose which button bar you wish to display, and use.

Additionally, you can add your own buttons to existing button bars. You can even incorporate menu items or features within the button bar of your choice. (Menu items are actions which are listed in WordPerfect's menu structure; features are additional actions which aren't.)

OTHER BUTTON BARS

1 Choose **View↳Button Bar Setup↳Select**. This calls up the Select Button Bar dialog box

2 Double-click the button bar you want displayed (or highlight it and choose Select)

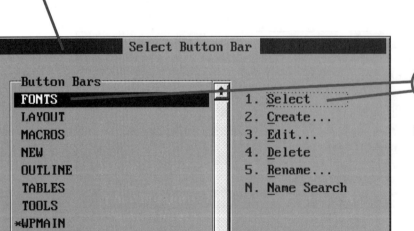

Choose Button Bar Setup from the View menu, then choose the Select sub-menu entry to call up the Select Button Bar dialog box

Highlight the Button Bar you need and choose Select

Highlight the button bar you want to add
new features to and click edit, to call up
the Edit Button Bar dialog box

ADDING NEW ICONS

3 Highlight the relevant
button bar in the Select
Button Bar dialog box and
click Edit. This calls up the
Edit Button Bar dialog box

4 Click Add Feature to insert
features as icons. This calls
up the Feature Button List
dialog box

5 WordPerfect provides a
drop-down list of features.
Double-click on the feature
you wish to add (or high-
light it and choose Select).
In the illustration, the
Writing Tools feature is
being added to the Fonts
button bar

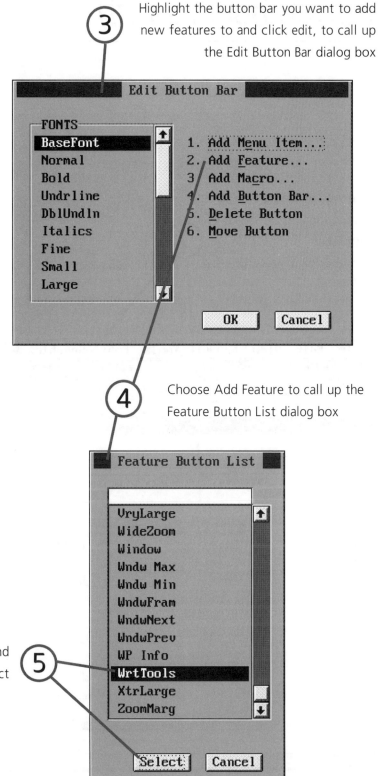

Choose Add Feature to call up the
Feature Button List dialog box

To add a feature, highlight it and
choose Select

25

Button bars (contd)

Basic steps:

6 Click on Add Menu Item in the Edit Button Bar dialog box to insert menu entries as icons

7 Pull down the relevant menu and double-click the appropriate option. In the illustration, the Cascade option from the Windows menu is being added to the Fonts button bar

Here we are adding the Cascade menu option to the WPMAIN button bar

⑦

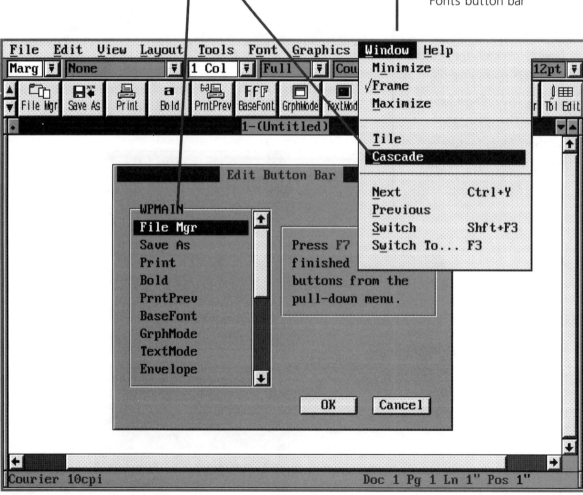

Document windows

WordPerfect 6 lets you have as many as nine document windows open at a time.

A document window is simply an on-screen *box* through which you can view a document. Any editing screen is essentially a window. However, it can often be useful to have more than one open at once. For instance, you could have two current windows, one featuring a document as it was prior to any editing changes, the other showing the ongoing document revisions... In this way, you can see precisely what changes have been made. The possibilities are almost endless.

WordPerfect's windows can be scaled and moved in a variety of ways. Although you can have up to nine open at once, you don't have to display them all at any given time; you can hide as many as you want.

This level of windows capability is normally associated with exclusively graphical programs. However, WordPerfect's windows display and operate fully in Text mode, as well as in Graphics and Page modes. Note, though, that the maximum window size depends on the other screen components (e.g. the Ribbon and button bars) which you've opted to display.

Document windows (contd)

Basic steps:

1 To resize the window *disproportionately*, place the mouse pointer on the left, right, top or bottom window border and drag the border in or out

2 To resize the window *proportionately*, place the mouse pointer on any corner and drag the corner in or out

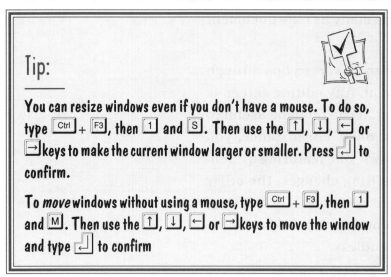

Tip:

You can resize windows even if you don't have a mouse. To do so, type `Ctrl` + `F3`, then `1` and `S`. Then use the `↑`, `↓`, `←` or `→` keys to make the current window larger or smaller. Press `↵` to confirm.

To *move* windows without using a mouse, type `Ctrl` + `F3`, then `1` and `M`. Then use the `↑`, `↓`, `←` or `→` keys to move the window and type `↵` to confirm

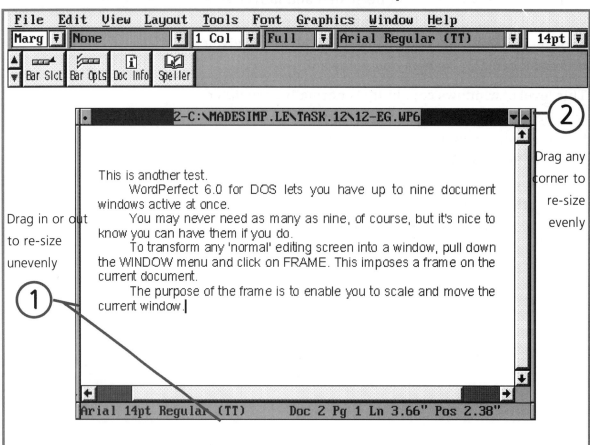

| File | Edit | View | Layout | Tools | Font | Graphics | Window | Help |

`Marg ▼` `None ▼` `1 Col ▼` `Full ▼` `Arial Regular (TT) ▼` `14pt ▼`

`Bar Slct` `Bar Opts` `Doc Info` `Speller`

2-C:\MADESIMP.LE\TASK.12\12-EG.WP6

This is another test.
WordPerfect 6.0 for DOS lets you have up to nine document windows active at once.
You may never need as many as nine, of course, but it's nice to know you can have them if you do.
To transform any 'normal' editing screen into a window, pull down the WINDOW menu and click on FRAME. This imposes a frame on the current document.
The purpose of the frame is to enable you to scale and move the current window.|

Drag any corner to re-size evenly

Drag in or out to re-size unevenly

Arial 14pt Regular (TT)   Doc 2 Pg 1 Ln 3.66" Pos 2.38"

28

3 To move the window to another location, place the mouse pointer on the title bar and drag the window

4 To *tile* document windows, choose
Window ⤷ Tile

Tip:
___

To switch to another window, simply click in it.

A very useful keyboard alternative is to press [Ctrl]+[Y] as many times as necessary. This cycles through available windows

This illustration shows three tiled windows

④ Bring down the Window menu and choose Tile

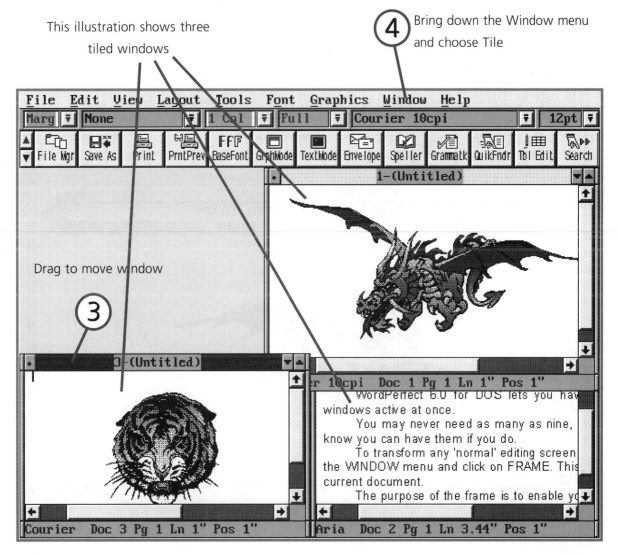

Drag to move window

③

Document windows (contd)

Basic steps:

Take note:

1 A window which fills the available editing screen is said to be *maximised*. Conversely, a *minimised* window occupies merely a small box on screen

2 Any window which is smaller than full-screen is automatically given a frame

5 To *cascade* document windows, choose
Window ↳ Cascade

Bring down the Window menu and choose Cascade

The three open windows are now cascaded

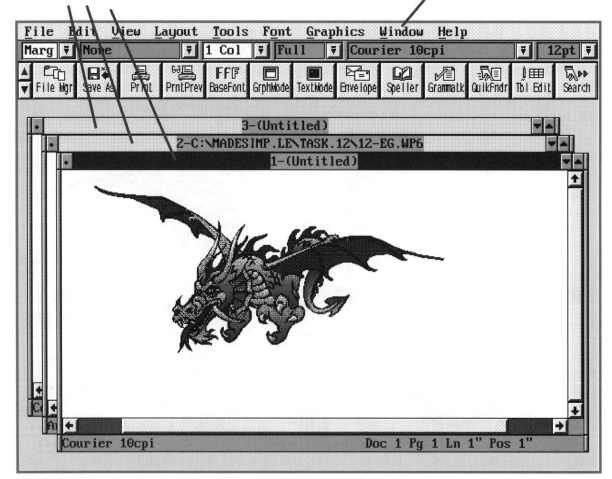

Formatting codes

All word processors use hidden formatting codes; they're generated and embedded within documents when you initiate text formatting operations (underlining, italicisation, and so on).

However, many programs don't make these codes obvious to users. WordPerfect 6 does, if you tell it to. You can opt to have formatting codes display in a special section of the editing screen.

Basic steps:

1 To make codes visible, choose **View↵Reveal Codes**. This launches the Reveal Codes window. To close the Reveal Codes window, repeat

2 To delete a code, click on it (or use the cursor keys to move the cursor over it) within the Reveal Codes window and press ⌫

Choose Reveal Codes
from the View menu

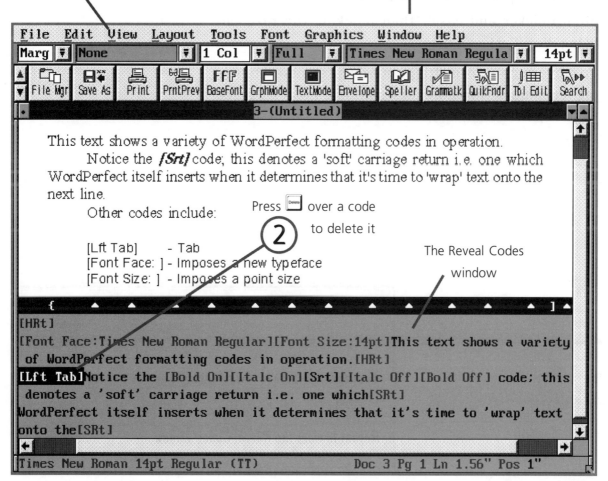

Press ⌫ over a code
to delete it

The Reveal Codes
window

Formatting codes (contd)

All WordPerfect codes are displayed in square brackets. Many codes appear in pairs. For instance, in the code window you might see:

[Bold On]**WordPerfect**[Bold Off]

Other codes appear singly. For example, [Hrt] on its own indicates a hard carriage-return (i.e. one which the user has imposed on text).

The advantage of working with codes is that you can edit them directly. For instance, if you've emboldened a word or phrase and want to reverse the operation, you can simply delete either of the two codes. This is often quicker and easier than blocking the text and using WordPerfect's menus.

To move or copy formatting codes, use standard blocking techniques (for more information on blocking, see page 70).

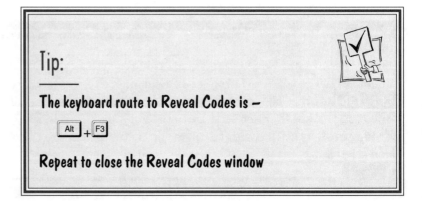

Tip:

The keyboard route to Reveal Codes is —

Alt + F3

Repeat to close the Reveal Codes window

Initial codes

All WordPerfect documents use embedded formatting codes.

You could, of course, simply insert the relevant codes into every document you work on. However, if a reasonable proportion of your documents share the same format and layout, you should use WordPerfect 6's Initial Codes feature.

There are two varieties — WordPerfect calls them Initial Codes Setup and Document Initial Codes — but the principle is identical.

Basic steps:

1 Choose
Layout➔Document.
This calls up the Document Format dialog box (over)

2 Click on Initial Codes Setup or Document Initial Codes. This calls up either the Initial Codes Setup dialog box, or the Document Initial Codes dialog box (see over)

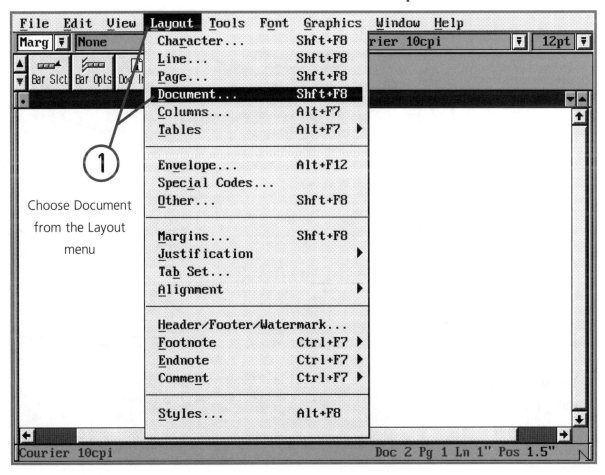

Choose Document from the Layout menu

Initial codes (contd)

Tip:

The keyboard routes to **Document Initial Codes** or **Initial Codes Setup** are, respectively

`Shift` + `F8` then `4` then `1`, and

`Shift` + `F8` then `4` then `2`

When you've finished, press `F7` and click **OK**, followed by **Close**

Choose Document Initial Codes or Initial Codes Setup

②

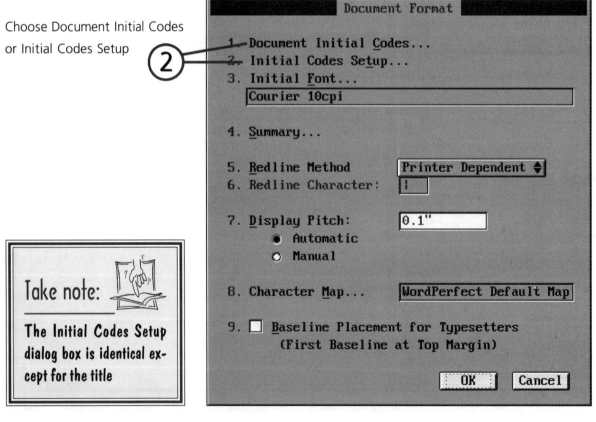

Document Format

1. Document Initial Codes...
2. Initial Codes Setup...
3. Initial Font...
   Courier 10cpi

4. Summary...

5. Redline Method — Printer Dependent ⬍
6. Redline Character: |

7. Display Pitch: 0.1"
   ● Automatic
   ○ Manual

8. Character Map... — WordPerfect Default Map

9. ☐ Baseline Placement for Typesetters
   (First Baseline at Top Margin)

OK   Cancel

Take note:

The Initial Codes Setup dialog box is identical except for the title

3 Use any of WordPerfect's menu or keyboard routes...

These codes determine language, text alignment and paper/size format: all prime candidates for inclusion in Initial Codes Setup

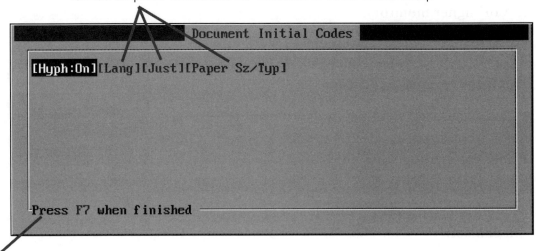

```
                    ┌─ Document Initial Codes ─┐
[Hyph:On][Lang][Just][Paper Sz/Typ]




└ Press F7 when finished ─────────────────────
```

4 Click here when done

Tip:

Use the Initial Codes Setup feature to preordain which formatting codes *every* new document you create will contain. Use Document Initial Codes to determine the codes which will apply throughout the *current* document.

Take note:

You can't press ⏎ or Esc to escape from the Document Initial Codes and Initial Codes Setup dialog boxes

Summary for Section 2

● Use Text mode for rapid text entry (and if you lack an EGA or higher monitor).

● Use Graphics and Page modes to work directly with graphics images. You can also use them (in conjunction with Print Preview – see page 138) for final proofing.

● You can use keystroke combinations or the mouse to move around the WordPerfect editing screen. Choose whichever method suits you.

● Use the Ribbon for immediate access to the most frequently used features with just a few mouse clicks. You can set:

- ❑ zoom levels
- ❑ styles
- ❑ column settings
- ❑ text justification
- ❑ typeface
- ❑ type size.

● Use the button bars to access commonly used features and menu commands.

● Use document windows to display more than one open document at once for ease of editing.

● Use the Reveal Codes window to see precisely what formatting codes are in force. You can also delete codes as a convenient way of disabling formatting options.

● Use Initial Codes options to specify which formatting options will apply automatically to documents.

3   File Manager

File Manager

WordPerfect 6 provides a centralised tool for performing disk management operations on files.

Some of these operations (the principal ones) are:

- opening documents
- inserting ('retrieving') documents
- printing documents.

We'll deal with these operations in detail, later. For the moment, though, we'll simply examine File Manager itself.

You can use File Manager to:

- copy, move and rename documents
- inspect documents (without opening them for editing)
- search for text within documents (without opening them for editing)
- search for document names
- print the File Manager list itself
- switch to alternative directories and create new directories
- specify one directory as the current default.

Basic steps:

1 Choose **File⇥File Manager**. This calls up the Specify File Manager List dialog box

2 Type in the name and path details of the directory whose contents you wish to display and click OK.

3 To specify a directory as the current default, type ⊟ before you enter the directory details. WordPerfect launches the Change Default Directory dialog box

4 Enter the directory details and click OK to confirm

5 Select the disk management function you require

6 Click Close when you've finished

① Choose File Manager from the File menu

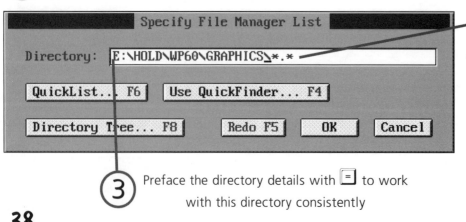

Type in details of the directory you want to view

③ Preface the directory details with ⊟ to work with this directory consistently

38

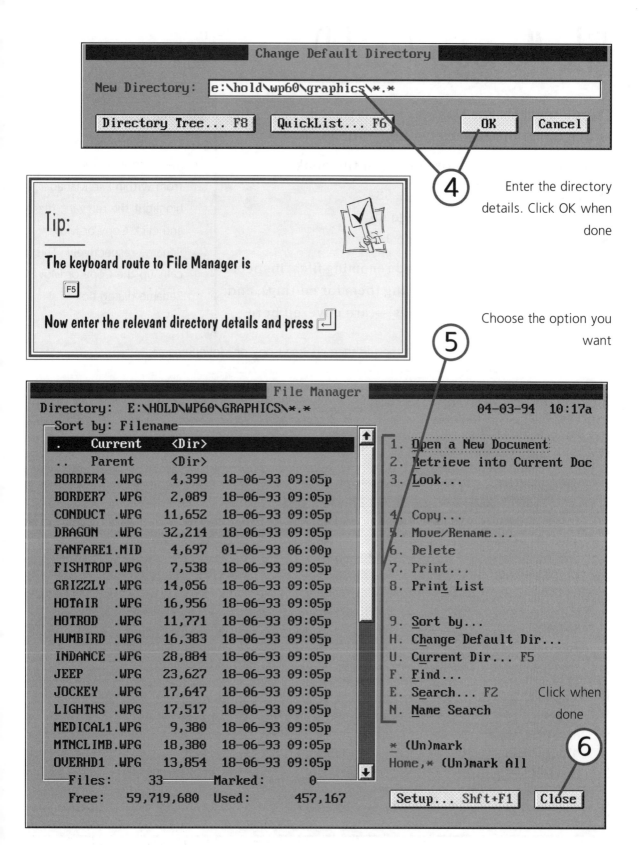

Change Default Directory

New Directory: `e:\hold\wp60\graphics\*.*`

[Directory Tree... F8] [QuickList... F6]   [OK] [Cancel]

④ Enter the directory details. Click OK when done

Tip:

The keyboard route to File Manager is

F5

Now enter the relevant directory details and press ↵

⑤ Choose the option you want

File Manager

Directory: E:\HOLD\WP60\GRAPHICS*.*   04-03-94 10:17a

Sort by: Filename

.	Current	‹Dir›
..	Parent	‹Dir›
BORDER4 .WPG	4,399	18-06-93 09:05p
BORDER7 .WPG	2,089	18-06-93 09:05p
CONDUCT .WPG	11,652	18-06-93 09:05p
DRAGON .WPG	32,214	18-06-93 09:05p
FANFARE1.MID	4,697	01-06-93 06:00p
FISHTROP.WPG	7,538	18-06-93 09:05p
GRIZZLY .WPG	14,056	18-06-93 09:05p
HOTAIR .WPG	16,956	18-06-93 09:05p
HOTROD .WPG	11,771	18-06-93 09:05p
HUMBIRD .WPG	16,383	18-06-93 09:05p
INDANCE .WPG	28,884	18-06-93 09:05p
JEEP .WPG	23,627	18-06-93 09:05p
JOCKEY .WPG	17,647	18-06-93 09:05p
LIGHTHS .WPG	17,517	18-06-93 09:05p
MEDICAL1.WPG	9,380	18-06-93 09:05p
MTNCLIMB.WPG	18,380	18-06-93 09:05p
OVERHD1 .WPG	13,854	18-06-93 09:05p

1. **O**pen a New Document
2. **R**etrieve into Current Doc
3. **L**ook...

4. **C**opy...
5. **M**ove/Rename...
6. **D**elete
7. **P**rint...
8. **P**rint List

9. **S**ort by...
H. C**h**ange Default Dir...
U. **C**urrent Dir... F5
F. **F**ind...
E. **S**earch... F2   Click when
N. **N**ame Search   done

* (Un)mark
Home,* (Un)mark All   ⑥

Files: 33   Marked: 0

Free: 59,719,680 Used: 457,167   [Setup... Shft+F1] [Close]

39

File Manager (contd)

WordPerfect 6's File Manager is a very useful base from which to perform a variety of operations.

Some of these are explored later in the book:

- opening documents — page 58
- retrieving document — page 60
- printing documents — page 144.

Others — copying, moving and renaming files, inspecting documents (without opening them for editing), and searching for document names — are covered here.

Basic steps:

COPYING OR MOVING

1 To copy or move documents to a new location from within File Manager, highlight the relevant file and click Copy or Move/Rename respectively. This calls up the Copy or Move/Rename dialog box

(1) Highlight the file then choose Copy or Move/Rename

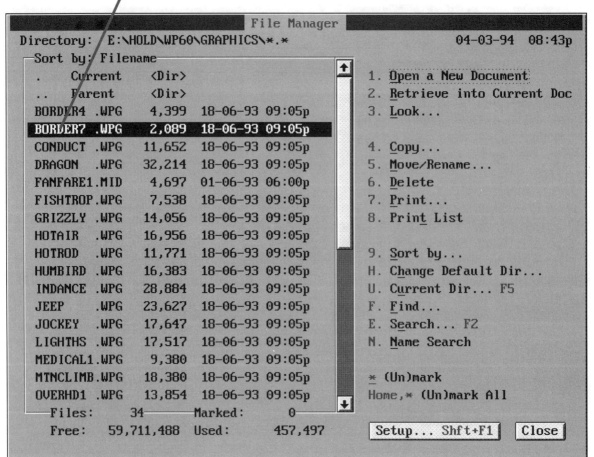

2 Enter the new directory
information (or the new
name, if the location is
unchanged)

3 Click OK to return to File
Manager

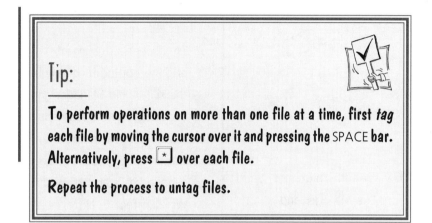

Tip:

To perform operations on more than one file at a time, first *tag*
each file by moving the cursor over it and pressing the SPACE **bar.**
Alternatively, press ⊡ over each file.

Repeat the process to untag files.

Enter the new directory or name ②

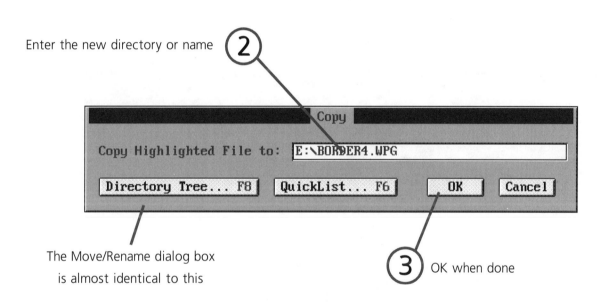

```
                        Copy

Copy Highlighted File to:  E:\BORDER4.WPG

[ Directory Tree... F8 ]  [ QuickList... F6 ]   [ OK ]   [ Cancel ]
```

The Move/Rename dialog box
is almost identical to this

③ OK when done

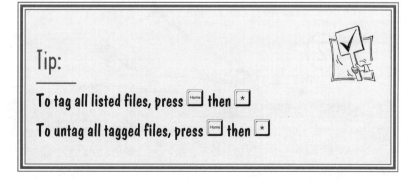

Tip:

To tag all listed files, press 🔲 then ⊡

To untag all tagged files, press 🔲 then ⊡

41

File Manager (contd)

INSPECTING

1 To inspect a document prior to editing it, highlight the file in File Manager and click Look. The document is viewed. The image shown is PENPUSH.WPG, supplied as standard with WordPerfect 6. Note, however, that what you

see is rather different for a text file

2 Click Next to view the following file, or select Previous to inspect the preceding file

3 Click Close when you've finished viewing the document

To view a file, highlight it in File Manager and click Look ①

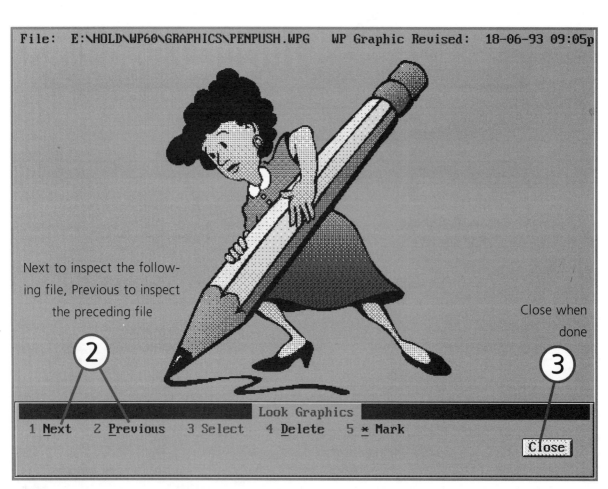

Next to inspect the following file, Previous to inspect the preceding file

Close when done

1 To locate a specific document from within the files currently listed within File Manager, click Search. This calls up the Search for Filename dialog box

2 Enter file name details then click Search to begin the searching operation

Note that when searching for files, you can use wildcards: '*' and '?'. The following examples should make these clear.

Searching for *.LTR would find all files with the suffix LTR, irrespective of how many letters are in the main title, and what they are.

JOHN*.L??, on the other hand, would locate all files whose name starts with JOHN (irrespective of whether or not there are any other letters after JOHN) *and* whose suffix starts with L followed by any two additional letters.

Choose search in the File Manager to look for files in the displayed directory

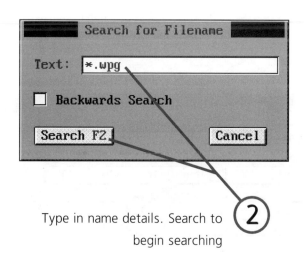

Type in name details. Search to begin searching

File Manager (contd)

Basic steps:

You can also use File Manager to:

● switch to alternative directories and create new directories

● specify one directory as the current File Manager default

● search for text *within* documents (without opening them for editing).

Text search (File Manager's *Find* option) isn't the same as searching for document names (*Search*). If you use the text search option, WordPerfect looks *inside* files rather than simply at their titles.

Find is a particularly useful option. You may, for instance, wish to trace a letter you've written to a specific contact. If the name you've given the document doesn't reflect the addressee, you can use Find to locate it.

CHANGING DIRECTORY

1 To switch to another directory using File manager, click Current Dir... This calls up the Specify File Manager List dialog box

2 Enter the new directory details and choose OK

① Choose Current Dir... in the File Manager

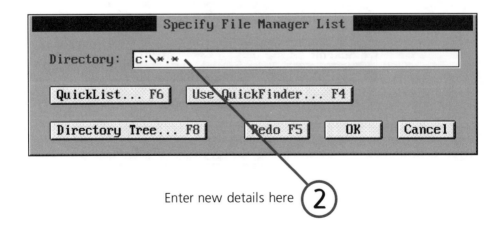

Enter new details here ②

1 To specify a directory as
the current default, click
Change Default Dir... This
calls up the Change default
Directory dialog box

2 Enter the directory details
and choose OK

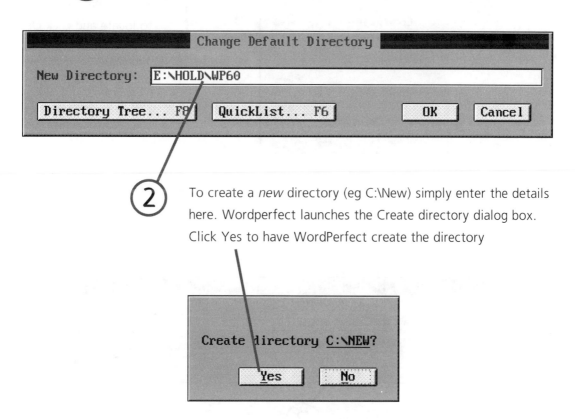

① Choose Change Default Dir...

Change Default Directory

New Directory: E:\HOLD\WP60

Directory Tree... F8   QuickList... F6   OK   Cancel

② To create a *new* directory (eg C:\New) simply enter the details
here. Wordperfect launches the Create directory dialog box.
Click Yes to have WordPerfect create the directory

Create directory C:\NEW?

Yes   No

File Manager (contd)

① Choose Find in File Manager

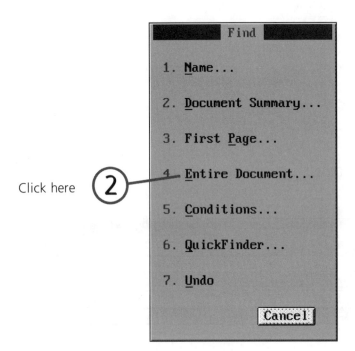

Click here ②

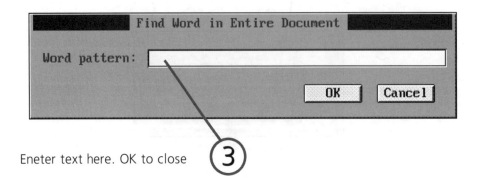

Eneter text here. OK to close ③

46

Directory Tree

Basic steps:

File Manager lets you view all files within a specific directory. However, it can often be useful to view the overall directory structure. This kind of overview makes it easier to navigate around your drives.

Use WordPerfect's Directory Tree to examine your general directory list. When you locate the appropriate directory, you can display it within File Manager.

1 Choose **File↳File Manager** to call up the Specify File Manager List dialog box

2 Click Directory Tree to call up the Directory Tree dialog box

① Choose File Manager from the File menu

Click here ②

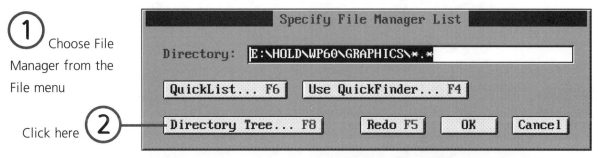

③

④

Highlight the new directory and choose Select Directory

To display a directory on another drive, click here

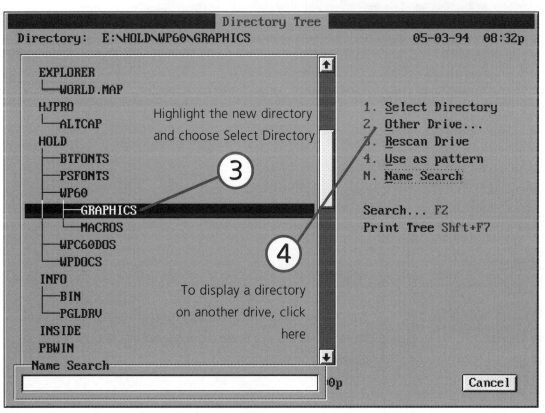

47

Directory tree (contd)

⑤ Choose the drive and click Select

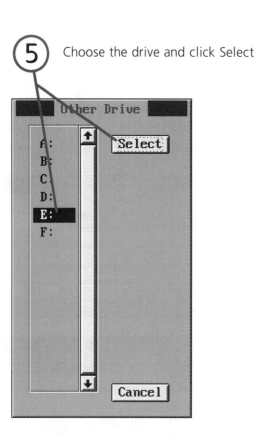

3 Highlight the new directory you need to display and click Select Directory. WordPerfect displays the directory within File Manager

4 If the new directory is on another drive, choose Other Drive — this calls up the Other Drive dialog box

5 Highlight the drive and choose Select. Now follow steps 3 and 4

Tip:

The keyboard route to Directory Tree is:

F5 then F8

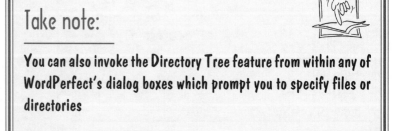

Take note:

You can also invoke the Directory Tree feature from within any of WordPerfect's dialog boxes which prompt you to specify files or directories

QuickList

Locating commonly used directories and files quickly can be a major problem on large hard disks. And large hard disks are now standard on many systems. For this reason, WordPerfect 6 provides QuickList.

QuickList is a more or less unique WordPerfect 6 feature which lets you allocate convenient *labels* quickly and easily to files and directories.

These labels are stored in a centralised list. Each label can hold up to forty characters (standard directory and file names, on the other hand, can only consist of a maximum of eight characters followed by a full stop and a maximum of three more). By selecting the label from within QuickList, you're instantly taken to the associated files and directories.

CREATING QUICKLIST ENTRIES

1 Choose **File→File Manager** to call up the Specify File Manager List dialog box

2 Select QuickList. This calls up the Quicklist dialog box (over)

(1) Choose File Manager from the File menu

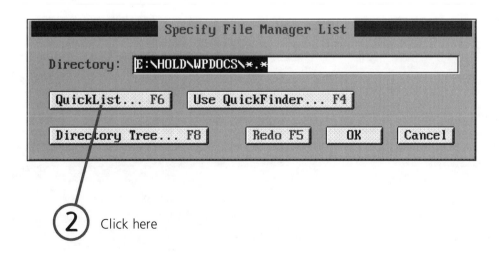

(2) Click here

49

QuickList (contd)

Tip:

The keyboard route to QuickList is

F5 then F6

3 Click Create to call up the Create QuickList Entry dialog box

4 Type in a description (for identification purposes) of the new QuickList entry

5 Enter the relevant directory path in the Filename/Directory field

6 Click OK when you've finished

③ Click here

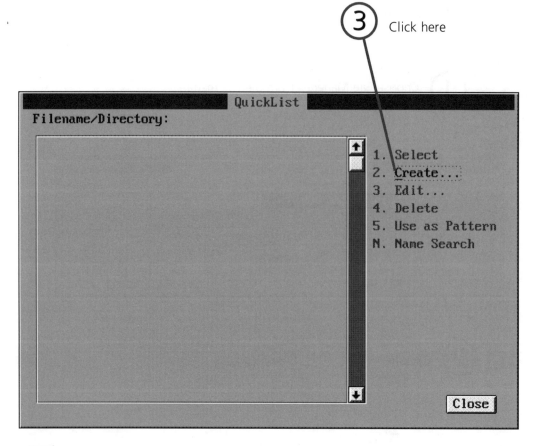

QuickList

Filename/Directory:

1. Select
2. Create...
3. Edit...
4. Delete
5. Use as Pattern
N. Name Search

Close

④ Describe the new QuickList entry

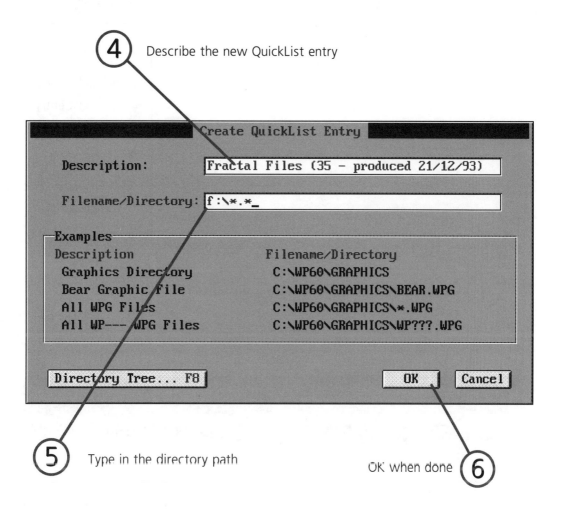

```
                    Create QuickList Entry

   Description:       Fractal Files (35 - produced 21/12/93)

   Filename/Directory: f:\*.*_

  ┌Examples───────────────────────────────────────────────┐
  │ Description                   Filename/Directory        │
  │  Graphics Directory            C:\WP60\GRAPHICS         │
  │  Bear Graphic File             C:\WP60\GRAPHICS\BEAR.WPG│
  │  All WPG Files                 C:\WP60\GRAPHICS\*.WPG   │
  │  All WP--- WPG Files           C:\WP60\GRAPHICS\WP???.WPG│
  └────────────────────────────────────────────────────────┘

   Directory Tree... F8                        OK      Cancel
```

⑤ Type in the directory path

⑥ OK when done

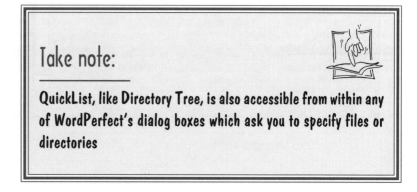

Take note:

QuickList, like Directory Tree, is also accessible from within any of WordPerfect's dialog boxes which ask you to specify files or directories

QuickList (contd)

Basic steps:

EDITING QUICKLIST ENTRIES

1 Highlight the appropriate QuickList entry

2 Click Edit

3 Adjust the Description and/ or Filename/Directory fields as appropriate

4 Click OK when done

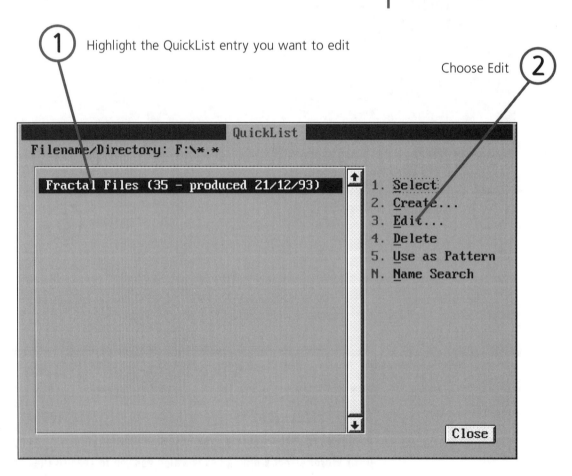

Highlight the QuickList entry you want to edit

Choose Edit

QuickList

Filename/Directory: F:*.*

Fractal Files (35 – produced 21/12/93)

1. Select
2. Create...
3. Edit...
4. Delete
5. Use as Pattern
N. Name Search

Close

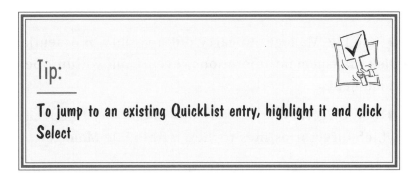

Tip:

To jump to an existing QuickList entry, highlight it and click
Select

③ Amend these fields as necessary

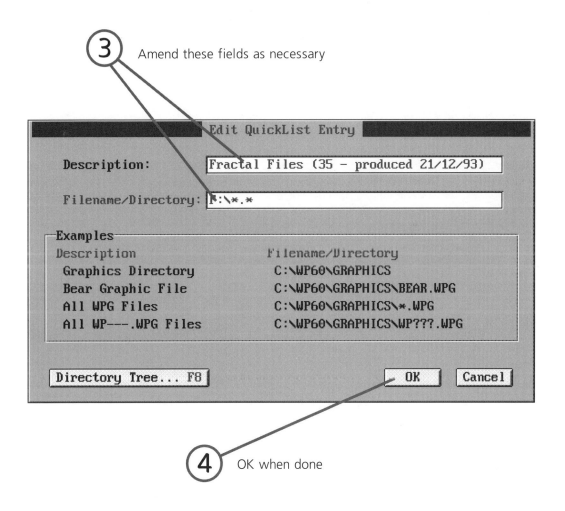

Edit QuickList Entry

Description: Fractal Files (35 – produced 21/12/93)

Filename/Directory: F:*.*

┌─Examples──┐
│ Description   Filename/Directory   │
│ Graphics Directory   C:\WP60\GRAPHICS   │
│ Bear Graphic File   C:\WP60\GRAPHICS\BEAR.WPG   │
│ All WPG Files   C:\WP60\GRAPHICS*.WPG   │
│ All WP───.WPG Files   C:\WP60\GRAPHICS\WP???.WPG   │
└───┘

[Directory Tree... F8]   [OK]   [Cancel]

④ OK when done

Summary for Section 3

● Use File Manager to carry out a variety of essential disk management operations, even from within open documents.

● Use Directory Tree as a convenient way to specify which directories/files to view within File Manager.

● Use QuickList to give often-used directories and files special titles. When you want to move to the associated directory or files, simply select the title within QuickList.

4 Working with documents

Creating a new document

Each time you run WordPerfect 6 a new, full-screen document window is automatically opened, with the editing cursor positioned in the top left-hand corner of the screen. This means that you can begin entering text immediately.

However, because WordPerfect permits as many as nine windows open simultaneously (if your computer has enough internal memory), there will be occasions when you'll need to open new documents manually.

Basic steps:

1 Choose **File⤷New**. This creates a new document

2 Alternatively, choose **Window⤷Switch To**. This calls up the Switch to Document dialog box

3 Click on any document number currently un-opened; WordPerfect opens it for you

① To create a new document, choose New from the File menu

② Or select Switch To from the Window menu to call up the Switch to Document dialog box

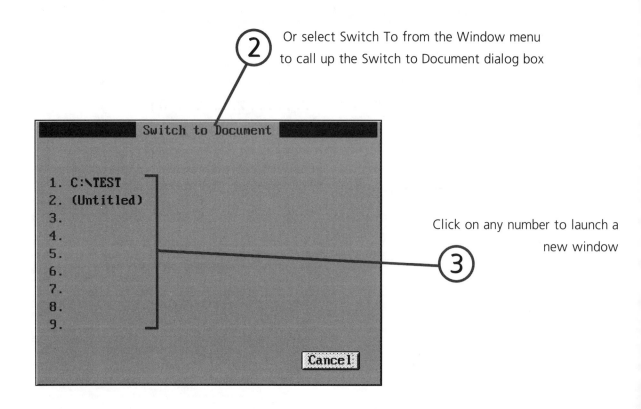

Click on any number to launch a new window

③

Take note:

You should distinguish between the following actions:

● Creating a new document and launching a new (that is, empty) window

● Opening a document and inserting an existing document into a new (empty) window (see page 58)

● Retrieving a document and inserting an existing document into a window which is already open (see page 60) and which may already contain text

Tip:

When you create a new document, WordPerfect automatically inserts the formatting codes specified with the Initial Codes Setup feature (for more information, see page 33)

Take note:

The keyboard route to the Switch to Document dialog box is:

⌂ then N

where N is the number of the new window you wish to open.

For instance, if you currently have only one window open, pressing ⌂ followed by 6 would launch a new window numbered 6

Opening documents

WordPerfect lets you open existing files into new windows.

As you're allowed to open as many as nine concurrent windows, opening existing documents is an operation you'll perform very often.

There are three principal ways in which you can do this. Use whichever method happens to be most suitable in any given situation.

Here are some hints.

- Step 2 can be particularly useful if the file you wish to open lies in the current default directory (for details of how to set the default directory, see page 38). If it does, simply enter the name without the directory path.
- Step 3 is the easiest, providing that the file you need to open has already been opened recently. WordPerfect maintains a list of the last four files opened. If you need to re-open one of these, you can simply select the list entry. If possible, use this method: it's much quicker.
- Step 4 is the basic method for opening existing documents when you need to locate them prior to opening them.

Tip:

The keyboard alternative to choosing File↳Open is

Shift + F10

Basic steps:

1. Choose **File↳Open**. This calls up the Open Document dialog box. Now use one of the following techniques
2. Enter the file name and directory path (if you know them). Make sure Open a New Document is selected. Click OK to load the file into a new window
3. If the file you need to open was opened within the last four documents, click the drop-down list button. Double-click the relevant file within the drop-down list to load it into a new window
4. If you don't know the directory path and file name, and the file hasn't recently been in use, click File Manager. Use File Manager's Search facility (see page 43) to locate the file. Then highlight it within File Manager and click Open a New Document

Take note:

Step 3 is only available if you're using a mouse

(1) Choose Open from the File menu

(2) Enter file and path details here. OK when done

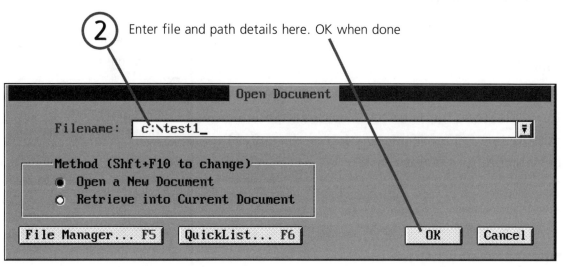

Click here for a list of recently opened files. Double-click on a file to load it (3)

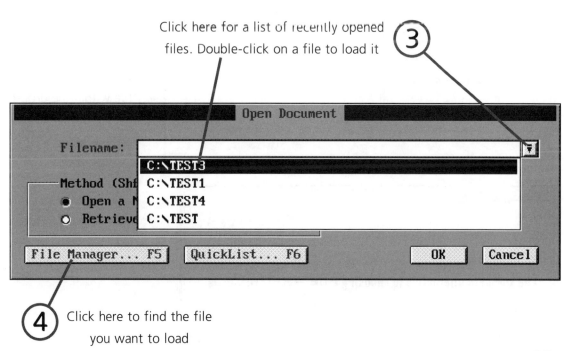

(4) Click here to find the file you want to load

Retrieving documents

WordPerfect gives an unusual title to the act of importing existing documents into an already current window. It calls this *retrieving*.

Retrieving is often useful as a way of combining two files into one. You open the first into a document window, move to the end (or, for that matter, any other appropriate location) and then retrieve the second document.

There are three principal ways you can do this. Use whichever method happens to be most suitable in any given situation. For more information on the suitability of these techniques, see page 58.

Take note:
_____
Step 3 is only available to you if you're using a mouse

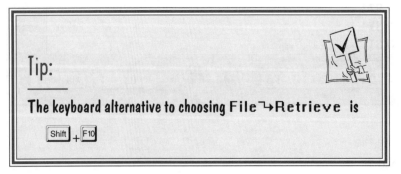

Tip:
_____
The keyboard alternative to choosing File↪Retrieve is

Shift + F10

1 Move the editing cursor to the correct juncture within the current window. Choose **File↪Retrieve**. This calls up the Retrieve Document dialog box. Now use one of the following techniques

2 Enter the file name and directory path (if you know them). Make sure Retrieve into Current Document is selected. Click OK to load the file into the host window

3 If the file you need to retrieve was opened within the last four documents, click ▼ to drop-down the drop-down list box. Double-click the relevant file within the drop-down list to retrieve it into the host window

4 If you don't know the directory path and file name, and the file hasn't recently been in use, click File Manager. Use File Manager's Name Search facility (see page 43) to locate the file. Then highlight it within File Manager and click Retrieve into Current Doc

(1) Choose Retrieve from the File menu

(2) Enter file and path details here. OK when done

```
███████████████ Retrieve Document ███████████████

   Filename:  ┌───────────────────────────────────────┬──┐
              │ c:\test1                                │▼ │
              └───────────────────────────────────────┴──┘

      ┌─Method (Shft+F10 to change)──────────────┐
      │  ○  Open a New Document                   │
      │  ●  Retrieve into Current Document        │
      └──────────────────────────────────────────┘

   ┌──────────────────┐  ┌──────────────────┐         ┌────────┐  ┌────────┐
   │ File Manager... F5│  │ QuickList... F6  │         │   OK   │  │ Cancel │
   └──────────────────┘  └──────────────────┘         └────────┘  └────────┘
```

(4) Click here to find the file you want to retrieve

Click here to retrieve a recent file (3)

Tip:

Make sure Retrieve into Current Document is selected

61

Non—WordPerfect files

You're not restricted just to opening and retrieving WordPerfect 6's own files. You can also open and retrieve documents produced by earlier versions of WordPerfect. Additionally, WordPerfect will automatically convert into its own format documents created by many other word processors. In the normal course of events, WordPerfect will recognise which program they come from: you simply have to confirm that WordPerfect's choice is correct.

You can reverse the process i.e. you can make WordPerfect save its files to disk in a form which can be read in by other word processors (see over for more information).

1 Go back to page 58 if you're opening a file, or to page 60 if you're retrieving it. Follow step 1 on either page then select and carry out the appropriate procedure

2 When it encounters a non–WordPerfect file, WordPerfect calls up the File Format dialog box before it converts the file

3 Make sure the correct file type is highlighted. If it is, click Select. WordPerfect converts the file

4 If the correct file type isn't automatically highlighted, scroll down the list. Highlight the relevant file type and click Select. WordPerfect then converts the file

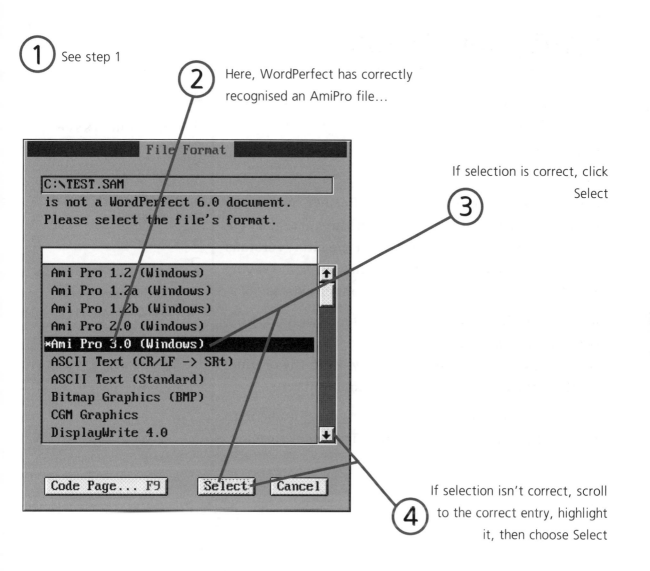

(1) See step 1

(2) Here, WordPerfect has correctly
recognised an AmiPro file...

If selection is correct, click
Select

(3)

File Format

C:\TEST.SAM
is not a WordPerfect 6.0 document.
Please select the file's format.

Ami Pro 1.2 (Windows)
Ami Pro 1.2a (Windows)
Ami Pro 1.2b (Windows)
Ami Pro 2.0 (Windows)
*Ami Pro 3.0 (Windows)
ASCII Text (CR/LF -> SRt)
ASCII Text (Standard)
Bitmap Graphics (BMP)
CGM Graphics
DisplayWrite 4.0

Code Page... F9   Select   Cancel

(4) If selection isn't correct, scroll
to the correct entry, highlight
it, then choose Select

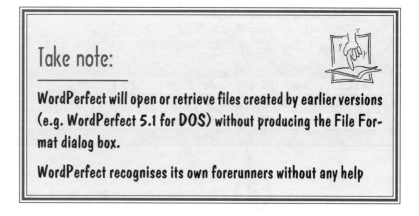

Take note:

**WordPerfect will open or retrieve files created by earlier versions
(e.g. WordPerfect 5.1 for DOS) without producing the File Format dialog box.**

WordPerfect recognises its own forerunners without any help

Saving documents

All amendments to documents must be saved to disk in order to be preserved. There are two methods:

- Save
- Save As.

When you save a document, WordPerfect overwrites the original file with the version in the current document window. Both the original, and the later, versions share the same name. This means that, after the saving operation, the original version no longer exists.

On the other hand, when you use the Save As option, WordPerfect saves the document as a separate file under a new name which you specify. Both the original and the later versions therefore remain intact.

Save As has one further advantage: you can use it to save existing files into other word processor formats.

1 Choose **File↵Save**. WordPerfect saves the contents of the current window under its original file name

2 Choose **File↵Save As**. This calls up the Save Document dialog box

3 Enter a new file name and the appropriate directory path details

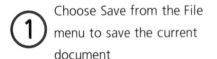

① Choose Save from the File menu to save the current document

② To Save As, choose this from the File menu

Save Document 2

Filename: `c:\new.wp6`

Format: WordPerfect 6.0

| Setup... Shft+F1 | Code Page... F9 |
| File List... F5 | QuickList... F6 | Password... F8 | OK | Cancel |

③ Enter file and directory details here

64

4 To save the file in the current window to another word processor format, click the drop-down list button ⬇. Double-click the correct file type in the resultant drop-down list

5 Click OK to save the contents of the current window under the new name

Click here to use another format. Double-click on the correct format

④

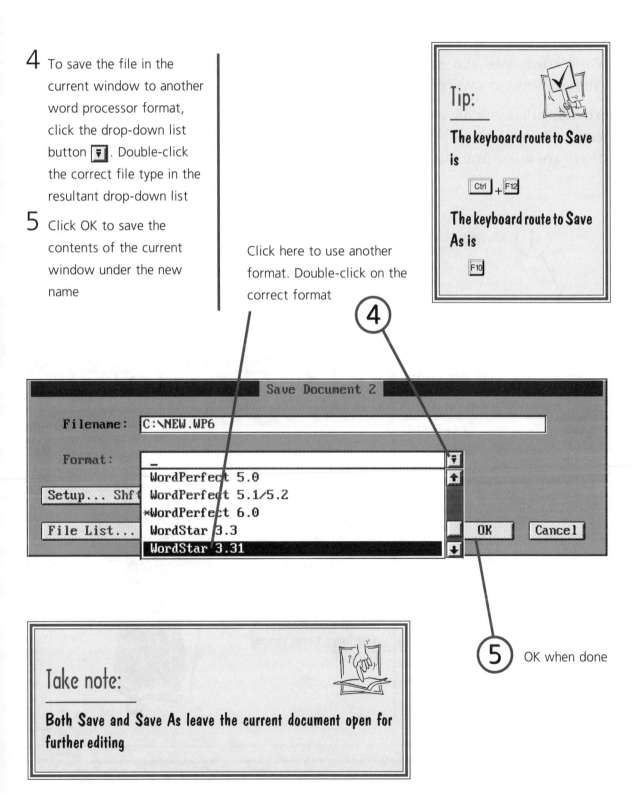

Tip:

The keyboard route to Save is

    Ctrl + F12

The keyboard route to Save As is

    F10

Save Document 2

Filename: C:\NEW.WP6

Format: _

| WordPerfect 5.0 |
| WordPerfect 5.1/5.2 |
| *WordPerfect 6.0 |
| WordStar 3.3 |
| WordStar 3.31 |

Setup... Shf

File List...

OK   Cancel

⑤ OK when done

Take note:

Both Save and Save As leave the current document open for further editing

Closing documents

WordPerfect lets you shut down current document windows without saving their contents to disk.

Providing that you haven't amended the window contents, this is the quickest way to leave a document (there are fewer prompts).

1 Choose **File ⊣ Close**. If the current document hasn't been revised, WordPerfect closes it immediately

2 If the current document *has* been amended since it was last saved, *and* you wish to save the full version (including the revisions) under a new

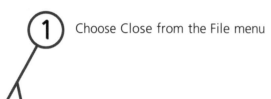

Choose Close from the File menu

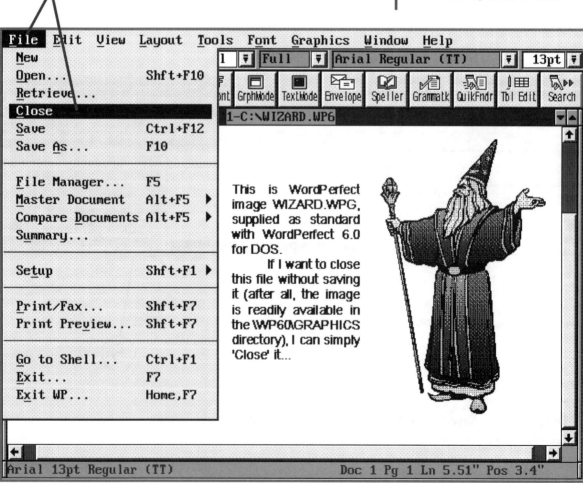

This is WordPerfect image WIZARD.WPG, supplied as standard with WordPerfect 6.0 for DOS.

If I want to close this file without saving it (after all, the image is readily available in the \WP60\GRAPHICS directory), I can simply 'Close' it...

name before closing it, click Save As. For more information on Save As, see page 64

3 If the current document has been amended since it was last saved, but you *don't* wish to save the full version (including the revisions) before closing it, click No

4 If the current document has been amended since it was last saved, and you *do* want to save the full version (including the revisions) under the original name before closing it, click Yes

5 Click Cancel if you decide not to close the document

If you *have* amended the contents since the last time the document was saved, WordPerfect provides a warning. You can then choose to:

● save the full document under a new name before closing it
● proceed with closing the document without saving it
● save the full document under the original name before closing it
● return to the document without closing or saving it.

Tip:

Get into the habit of saving your files before you close them to avoid losing your work

Click here to save under a new name

Click here to discard editing changes

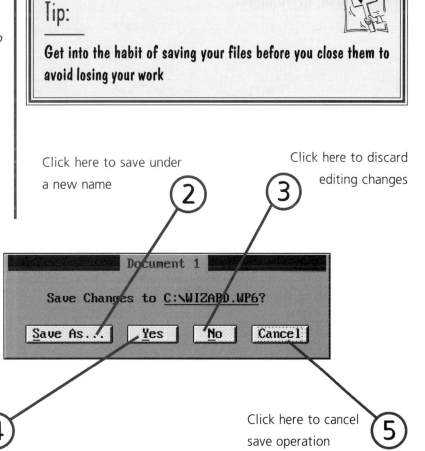

Click here to save under the original name

Click here to cancel save operation

Summary for Section 4

Use Section 4 to learn how to:

● Create new documents.

● Load existing documents into new document windows.

● Load existing documents into windows which already contain text.

● Convert documents in third–party formats into WordPerfect documents.

● Save documents to disk in WordPerfect's own format (and in third-party formats).

● Shut down documents.

5 Working with text

Blocking text

WordPerfect 6 makes working with text easy and straightforward.

For one thing, you can begin entering text immediately after you've loaded WordPerfect because it opens a new document window automatically. Simply begin typing in text...

However, once you've inserted the text, you may well need to perform a variety of operations on it. These include:

- formatting enhancements (underlining, bold, italics, and so on)
- copy, cut and paste operations
- deleting and undeleting text
- font and type size changes
- justification changes
- line spacing adjustments
- the imposition of automatic hyphenation
- the imposition of borders.

One easy way to implement these is to *block* the relevant sections of text before invoking the operations. Blocking text simply tells WordPerfect which sections of text to revise.

TO BLOCK TEXT...

1 Position the editing cursor at the start of the text you wish to block

2 Choose **Edit**↳**Block**

3 Use the cursor keys to move the cursor to the end of the relevant section of text. You can also use the ⌨Home, ⌨End, ⌨Page Up and ⌨Page Down keys to travel through text more rapidly

4 WordPerfect blocks the text. You can now apply the relevant enhancements (see subsequent pages)

Tip:

You can also use the mouse to block text. Position the mouse cursor at the start of the relevant text. Click and hold down the left button. Drag the cursor to the end of the text and release the button

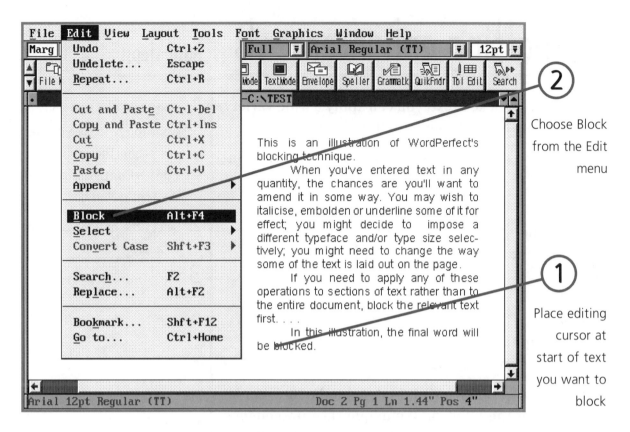

Choose Block from the Edit menu

Place editing cursor at start of text you want to block

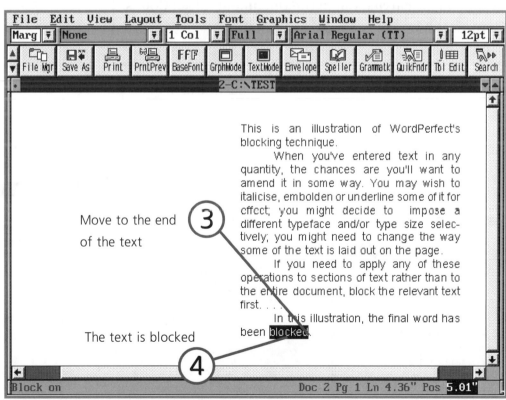

Move to the end of the text

The text is blocked

Formatting enhancements

Once you've blocked text, you can apply a wide variety of formatting enhancements to it.

WordPerfect calls these *font attributes*, and they include:

- bold
- underline
- double underline
- italics
- outline
- shadow
- small capitals
- typefaces and type sizes.

Note that any subsequent font amendments implemented with the blocking technique take precedence over changes carried out in the Document Initial Codes feature.

Basic steps:

1 First block the text you want to revise (see previous page). Then choose **Font↳Font**. This calls up the Font dialog box

2 Select the option you want to apply

3 Click OK

In this example we'll change the font and size of some text

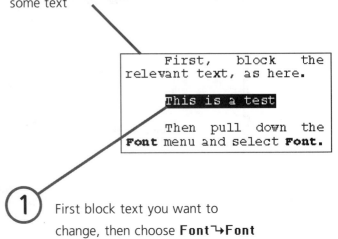

```
    First,    block    the
relevant text, as here.

This is a test

    Then   pull   down   the
Font menu and select Font.
```

① First block text you want to change, then choose **Font↳Font**

Tip:

The keyboard route to the Font dialog box is

[Ctrl] + [F8]

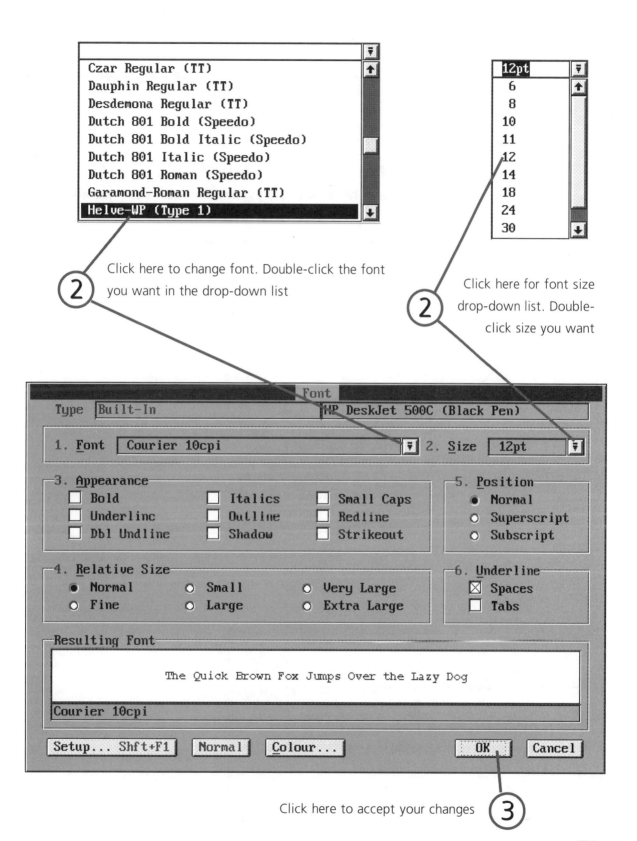

Czar Regular (TT)
Dauphin Regular (TT)
Desdemona Regular (TT)
Dutch 801 Bold (Speedo)
Dutch 801 Bold Italic (Speedo)
Dutch 801 Italic (Speedo)
Dutch 801 Roman (Speedo)
Garamond-Roman Regular (TT)
Helve-WP (Type 1)

12pt
6
8
10
11
12
14
18
24
30

② Click here to change font. Double-click the font you want in the drop-down list

② Click here for font size drop-down list. Double-click size you want

Font

Type Built-In   HP DeskJet 500C (Black Pen)

1. **F**ont   Courier 10cpi   2. **S**ize   12pt

3. **A**ppearance
☐ Bold   ☐ Italics   ☐ Small Caps
☐ Underline   ☐ Outline   ☐ Redline
☐ Dbl Undline   ☐ Shadow   ☐ Strikeout

5. Position
● Normal
○ Superscript
○ Subscript

4. **R**elative Size
● Normal   ○ Small   ○ Very Large
○ Fine   ○ Large   ○ Extra Large

6. **U**nderline
☒ Spaces
☐ Tabs

Resulting Font

The Quick Brown Fox Jumps Over the Lazy Dog

Courier 10cpi

[Setup... Shft+F1] [Normal] [Colour...]   [OK] [Cancel]

Click here to accept your changes ③

Blocked text is reformatted with the enhancements you specify (a new font and size, in this example) in the Font dialog box

> First,   block   the
> relevant text, as here.
>
> ## This is a test
>
> Then   pull   down   the
> **Font** menu and select **Font.**

Format enhancement could equally be emboldening (as here) or italics, underline, superscript, subscript, and so on

Copy, cut and paste

WordPerfect provides techniques for copying and moving blocks of text.

These techniques are:

- copy
- cut
- paste
- copy and paste
- cut and paste.

Use *copy* to copy blocked text into WordPerfect's *buffer*. The buffer is a section of computer memory used for temporary storage. The original text is left intact. You can then *paste* (see later) the copy into the same, or another, document on demand.

Cut is identical to copy with one exception: the original text is erased.

COPY, CUT AND PASTE

1 First block the relevant text. Then choose **Edit⤷Copy** or **Edit⤷Cut**

Block the text, then choose
Edit⤷Copy, or **Edit⤷Cut**

Here we're going to move this blocked section of text down to the bottom

```
This   illustrates   copying   and
moving operations.
       Let's  say  we  want  to  move
the   following   text   to   another
location:
       WordPerfect makes it easy to
move text
       How   do   we   go   about   it?
First,  block  the  relevant  text
(see above).
       Then pull down the Edit menu
and click on cut.
```

Copy, cut & paste (contd)

Paste inserts buffer text into a document at the location of the editing cursor.

Copy and paste is a joint operation. It copies the blocked text and pastes it back into a new location, all in one operation. Use this for convenience.

Cut and paste is equivalent to moving text, i.e. the original text is deleted, copied into the buffer, then pasted back into a new location. Use this for convenience.

Note that WordPerfect's buffer can only hold one block of text at a time. However, it retains this until:

● you place more text in it, or
● you close down WordPerfect.

② Choose Paste from the Edit menu

```
This    illustrates    copying    and
moving operations.
        Let's say we want to move
the  following  text  to  another
location▮

        How  do  we  go  about  it?
First,  block  the  relevant  text
(see above).
        Then pull down the **Edit** menu
and click on **Cut.**
        The text 'disappears'. Now
move  the  cursor  to  the  new
location. Pull down the **Edit** menu
again  and  click  on  **Paste.**  The
text is pasted in▮

WordPerfect makes it easy to move
text
```

The text is pasted in at the correct location

Copy and Paste, and Cut and Paste

3 Block the relevant text, then choose **Edit→Copy and Paste** or **Edit→Cut and Paste**

4 Move the cursor to the new location then press ↵ to insert the text

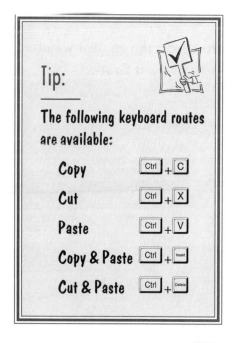

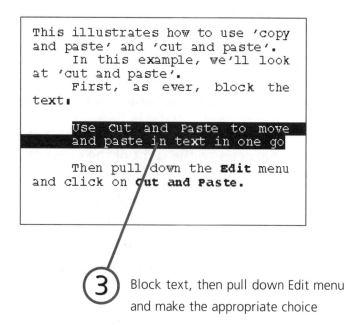

```
This illustrates how to use 'copy
and paste' and 'cut and paste'.
     In this example, we'll look
at 'cut and paste'.
     First, as ever, block the
text:

     Use Cut and Paste to move
     and paste in text in one go

     Then pull down the Edit menu
and click on Cut and Paste.
```

3 Block text, then pull down Edit menu and make the appropriate choice

```
This illustrates how to use 'copy
and paste' and 'cut and paste'.
     In this example, we'll look
at 'cut and paste'.
     First, as ever, block the
text:



     Now pull down the Edit menu
and click on Cut and Paste.
     The text is erased. Position
the cursor at the new location
and press RETURN. The text is
pasted in:

     Use Cut and Paste to move
     and paste in text in one go

     Voilà!
```

4 At the new location, press ↵

Tip:

The following keyboard routes are available:

Copy	Ctrl + C
Cut	Ctrl + X
Paste	Ctrl + V
Copy & Paste	Ctrl + Insert
Cut & Paste	Ctrl + Delete

Deleting text

WordPerfect provides a variety of key combinations which help with the job of deleting sections of text.

You can, of course, simply use the ⌫ and ⌫ keys. ⌫ erases one character to the right of the cursor, unless you're working in Text mode when it erases the character under the cursor. ⌫, on the other hand, deletes one character to the left. If you hold these keys down, WordPerfect will remove successive characters fairly rapidly. But there are quicker, easier and more convenient ways to delete text.

Position the cursor in the first word which requires to be deleted. Then the following combinations should prove useful:

- Ctrl + Delete erases the entire word
- Ctrl + Backspace erases the entire word
- Ctrl + End erases from the cursor to the end of the line
- Ctrl + Page Down erases from the cursor to the end of the page

However, the easiest way to delete text in any quantity is to block it first...

1 Block the text to be deleted (see page 70 for a discussion of blocking techniques)

2 Press Delete or Backspace. The entire block is erased.

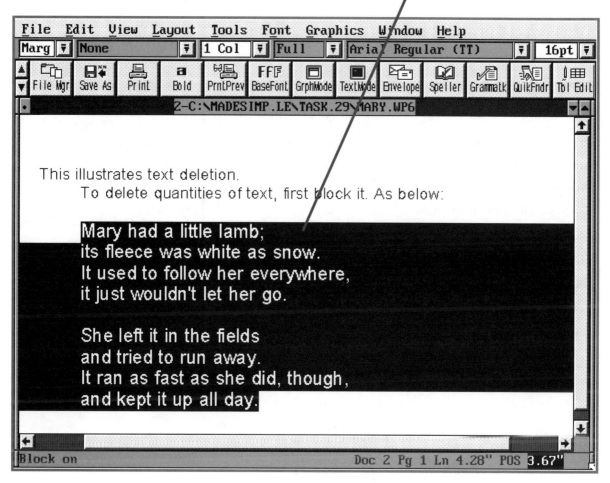

Block the text you want to delete

This illustrates text deletion.
    To delete quantities of text, first block it. As below:

Mary had a little lamb;
its fleece was white as snow.
It used to follow her everywhere,
it just wouldn't let her go.

She left it in the fields
and tried to run away.
It ran as fast as she did, though,
and kept it up all day.

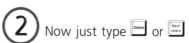

Now just type ⌫ or ⌫

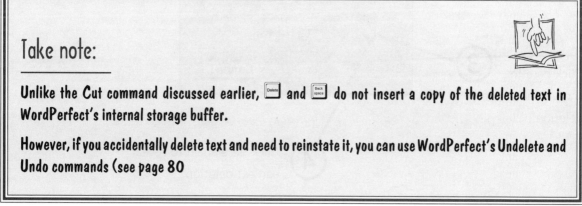

Take note:

Unlike the Cut command discussed earlier, ⌫ and ⌫ do not insert a copy of the deleted text in WordPerfect's internal storage buffer.

However, if you accidentally delete text and need to reinstate it, you can use WordPerfect's Undelete and Undo commands (see page 80

Undelete & undo

WordPerfect 6 provides two methods for restoring deleted text.

- Use Undo to restore text to its original location.
- Use Undelete to restore text to another location.

There is a further difference. Undelete retains full details of the last three deleted text sections, so you can choose which section to reinstate. Undo, however, only restores the last deletion.

You can also use Undo to reverse a wide variety of editing operations. For instance, you can undo:

- blocking operations
- amendments to font attributes
- margin amendments
- and even undeletions.

Basic steps:

USING UNDELETE

1 Position the cursor at the location to which you want the deleted text restored. Choose **Edit↳Undelete**. This calls up the Undelete dialog box

2 To restore the last deleted text, click Restore

3 To restore the next-to-last deleted text, click Previous Deletion. WordPerfect highlights the text on screen

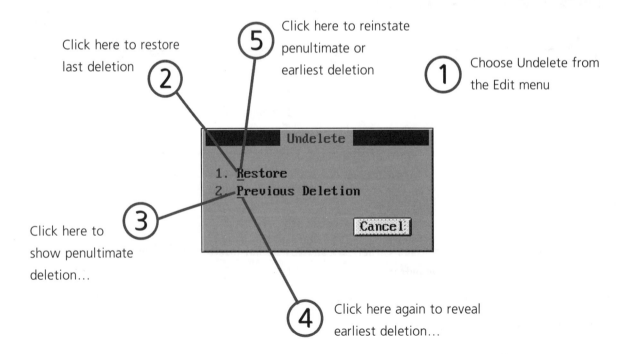

Click here to restore last deletion ②

Click here to reinstate penultimate or earliest deletion ⑤

Choose Undelete from the Edit menu ①

Click here to show penultimate deletion... ③

Click here again to reveal earliest deletion... ④

Undelete
1. Restore
2. Previous Deletion
Cancel

4 If necessary, click Previous Deletion again to display the text which was deleted before this

5 Click Restore to reinstate the text revealed by Steps 3 or 4

USING UNDO

6 To reverse the previous editing action, choose **Edit⤳Undo**

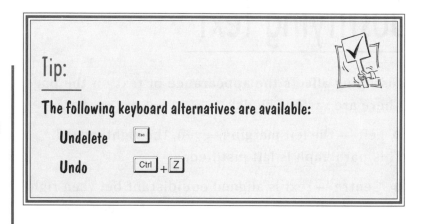

Tip:

The following keyboard alternatives are available:

Undelete `Esc`

Undo `Ctrl` + `Z`

⑥ Click here to Undo the last editing action

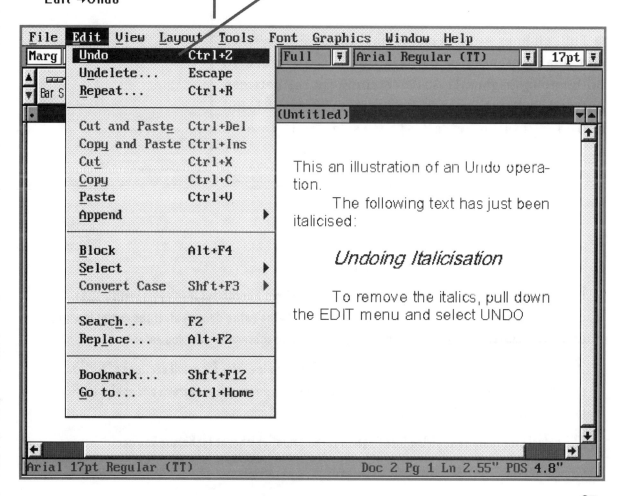

File　Edit　View　Layout　Tools　Font　Graphics　Window　Help

Undo	Ctrl+Z
Undelete...	Escape
Repeat...	Ctrl+R
Cut and Paste	Ctrl+Del
Copy and Paste	Ctrl+Ins
Cut	Ctrl+X
Copy	Ctrl+C
Paste	Ctrl+V
Append	▶
Block	Alt+F4
Select	▶
Convert Case	Shft+F3 ▶
Search...	F2
Replace...	Alt+F2
Bookmark...	Shft+F12
Go to...	Ctrl+Home

Marg　Full ▼ Arial Regular (TT) ▼ 17pt ▼

(Untitled)

This an illustration of an Undo operation.

The following text has just been italicised:

Undoing Italicisation

To remove the italics, pull down the EDIT menu and select UNDO

Arial 17pt Regular (TT)　　Doc 2 Pg 1 Ln 2.55" POS 4.8"

Justifying text

Justifying affects the appearance of text on the page. There are various kinds:

● Left — the left margin is even, the right jagged. This paragraph is left justified.

●   Centre — text is aligned equidistant between right and left margins. This paragraph is centred.

●   Right — the right margin is even, the left jagged. This paragraph is right justified.

● Full — both the left and right margins are even. This paragraph is full justified (normally just called justified).

● Full, all lines — a special format for headings/titles and final sentences of paragraphs. Text is forced to both left and right margins stretching spaces between letters as evenly as possible to fit. This paragraph is full a l l   l i n e s   j u s t i f i e d

Basic steps:

1 Place the cursor at the relevant location within a document. Choose **Layout↳Justification**

2 Choose the justification type from the sub-menu

Take note:

There are two basic techniques of justification

1 You can position the cursor at the relevant location within a document then apply justification. If you do this at the start of a document, justification applies to the entire document. If the cursor is within a paragraph, however, it only applies to that paragraph, and subsequent text you enter

2 You can block the text you wish to justify first. Blocking is easier for small sections of text, and it's much more precise. For instance, if you block one line within an overall paragraph and apply justification to it, the effect is limited to that line

The actual procedure of applying justification is the same, whichever technique you use

82

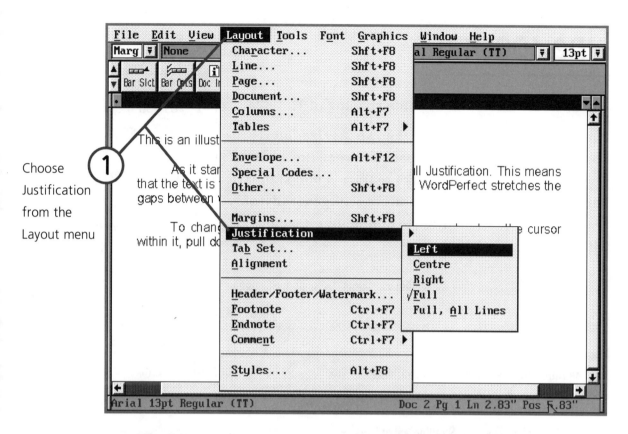

Choose
Justification
from the
Layout menu

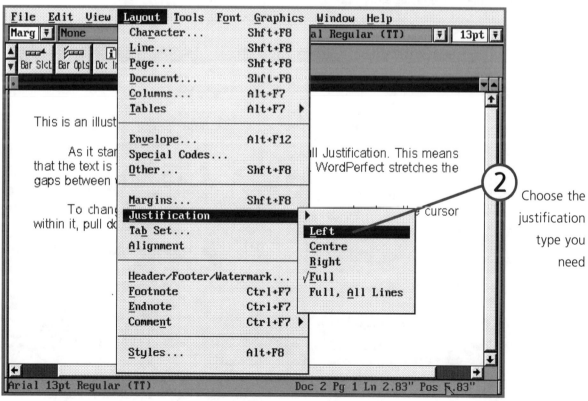

Choose the
justification
type you
need

Line spacing

WordPerfect 6 defaults to a line spacing of 1.

Line spacing — sometimes known as *leading* (pronounced *ledding*) — is the space between lines of text. Certain word processing tasks require a non-standard line spacing. For instance, editors will generally only read manuscripts submitted in double-line spacing (i.e. with a line spacing of 2).

Basic steps:

1 Position the cursor at the point from which you want to change line spacing, or block the text to be changed

2 Choose **Layout↦Line**. This calls up the Line Format dialog box

3 Click Line Spacing and enter a new figure in the number box

4 Click OK

Tip:

The following keyboard route is available:

Shift + F8 to call up the Line Format dialog box, then

L to select the Line Spacing entry box

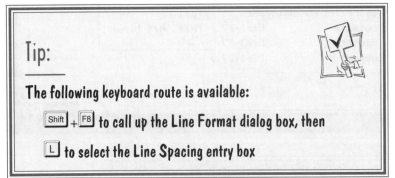

(1) See step 1

(2) Choose Line from the Layout menu

(3) Click here, then enter the new line spacing

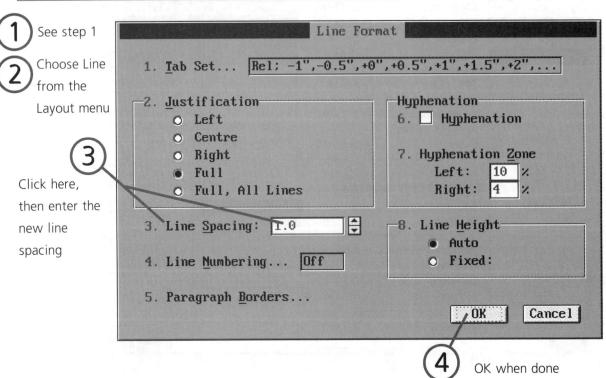

Line Format

1. <u>T</u>ab Set... Rel: −1",−0.5",+0",+0.5",+1",+1.5",+2",...

2. <u>J</u>ustification
- ○ Left
- ○ Centre
- ○ Right
- ● Full
- ○ Full, All Lines

Hyphenation

6. ☐ <u>H</u>yphenation

7. Hyphenation Zone
    Left: [10] %
    Right: [4] %

3. Line <u>S</u>pacing: [1.0] ⬍

4. Line <u>N</u>umbering... Off

5. Paragraph <u>B</u>orders...

8. Line Height
- ● Auto
- ○ Fixed:

[OK] [Cancel]

(4) OK when done

Hyphenation

If text is subject to full justification (see page 82), WordPerfect increases gaps between words to force lines flush with left and right margins. The effect is sometimes unattractive to the eye. This is more likely to be the case if the text is laid out in columns or narrow margins, or if large words are present.

To get round this difficulty, you can make WordPerfect hyphenate text automatically.

You can control the degree of hyphenation, too. WordPerfect uses a *hot zone* approach. Any words within the hot zone (located on and around the right text margin) are hyphenated.

The first paragraph in this selection of text is not hyphenated automatically. Because of this, the second line letter spacing gives an unattractive appearance

The final paragraph, on the other hand — the first paragraph repeated — is automatically hyphenated, so the line breaks more naturally with a hyphenated word

This illustrates the effect of implementing automatic hyphenation.

In this example, automatic hyphenation is not yet in force. This has resulted in line 2 looking relatively offputting: there is too big a gap between 'of' & 'implementing'...

Below is a copy of the first paragraph with hyphenation in force:

This illustrates the effect of implementing automatic hyphenation.

Hyphenation (contd)

Tip:

To amend the hyphenation hot zone, select Hyphenation Zone in the Line Format dialog box. Insert higher figures in the Left and Right entry fields to produce fewer hyphenated words. Insert lower figures to increase the extent of hyphenation

AUTOMATIC HYPHENATION

1 Position the cursor at the location from which you wish to turn automatic hyphenation on or off

2 Choose **Layout⤷Line**. This calls up the Line Format dialog box

3 Check the Hyphenation check box to turn it on, uncheck it to turn it off

4 Click OK to confirm

(1) See step 1

(2) Choose Line from the Layout menu

(3) Click here

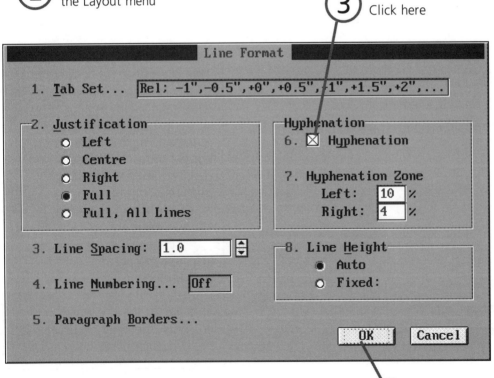

(4) OK when done

HYPHENATION CONFIRMATION

1 Choose **File↳Setup**.
Choose Environment from
the sub-menu. This calls up
the Environment dialog box

2 Click Prompt for Hyphenation. Select either Always
or When Required from the
drop-down list

3 Click OK to confirm

You can also make WordPerfect prompt you for confir-
mation before it hyphenates... There are three options:

● Never
● Always
● When Required.

If *always* or *when required* are selected, WordPerfect
produces a series of options when it encounters a word
it thinks should be hyphenated. Simply make the appropriate choice.

Choose Setup from the File menu

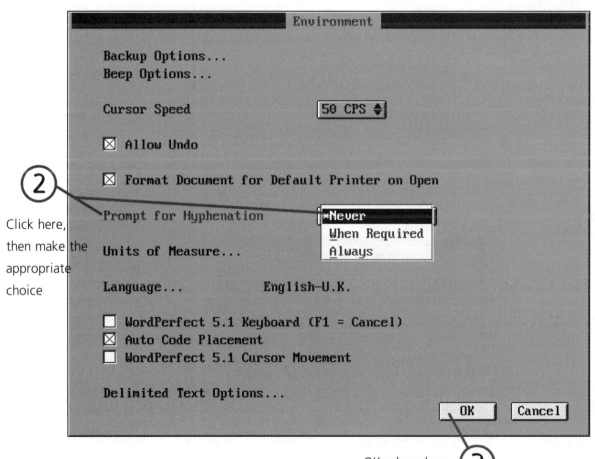

Click here,
then make the
appropriate
choice

OK when done ③

Text borders

It can often be useful to surround text with a border.

For instance, business letters can look more effective with a suitable page border: it attracts the eye. And individual paragraphs within a document can have more impact if bordered. Optionally, you can also fill the area within a text border with a pattern.

WordPerfect lets you apply borders to paragraphs, columns, whole pages and blocked text. Text borders are linked to WordPerfect's powerful *styles* feature (for more information on styles, see Section 8).

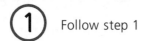 Follow step 1

Basic steps:

APPLYING TEXT BORDERS

1 Block the text to which you wish to apply the border (this is the easiest and most precise method). Or place the cursor within the paragraph, column or page from which the border should apply

2 Choose
   Graphics↳Borders.
   Select Paragraph, Page or Column from the sub-menu. This calls up the Create Paragraph, Page, or Column Border dialog boxes respectively

You can apply borders of varying widths and types to paragraphs

> This paragraph has had the following border style applied: 'Thick Thin Border'. It has also been filled. The fill style used is: '30% Shaded Fill'

Similarly, you can apply various fills within the borders

88

3 Click Border Style. This calls up the Border Styles dialog box (see step 6 over for details)

4 If you want the area inside your text border to be filled, click Fill Style. This calls up the Fill Styles dialog box (see step 7 over for details)

5 Click OK to confirm

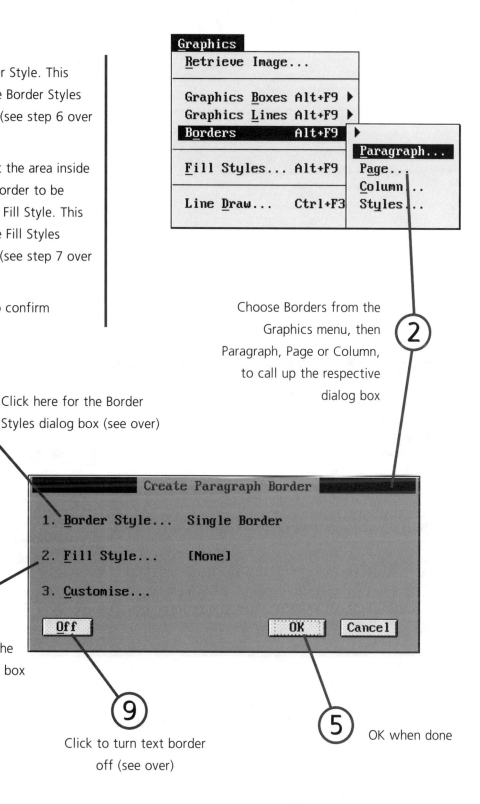

Graphics
Retrieve Image...

Graphics **B**oxes Alt+F9 ▶
Graphics **L**ines Alt+F9 ▶
Borders   Alt+F9 ▶

Paragraph...
Page...
Column...
St**y**les...

Fill Styles... Alt+F9

Line **D**raw...   Ctrl+F3

Choose Borders from the Graphics menu, then Paragraph, Page or Column, to call up the respective dialog box

(2)

Click here for the Border Styles dialog box (see over)

(3)

Create Paragraph Border

1. **B**order Style...   Single Border

2. **F**ill Style...   [None]

3. **C**ustomise...

Off   OK   Cancel

(4)

Click here for the Fill Style dialog box (see page 91)

(9)

Click to turn text border off (see over)

(5)

OK when done

Text borders (contd)

Border Styles dialog box (called up with step 3 on page 89)

6 Double-click the appropriate border style (or highlight it and click Select)

7 Double-click the appropriate fill style (or highlight it and click Select)

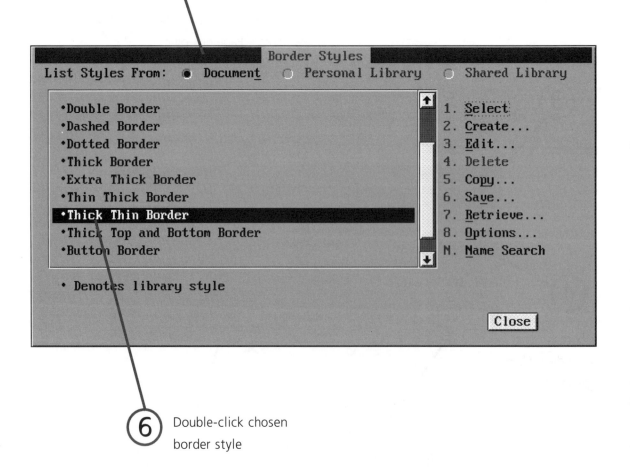

Border Styles

List Styles From: ● Document   ○ Personal Library   ○ Shared Library

•Double Border
•Dashed Border
•Dotted Border
•Thick Border
•Extra Thick Border
•Thin Thick Border
•Thick Thin Border
•Thick Top and Bottom Border
•Button Border

* Denotes library style

1. Select
2. Create...
3. Edit...
4. Delete
5. Copy...
6. Save...
7. Retrieve...
8. Options...
N. Name Search

Close

6 Double-click chosen border style

DISABLING TEXT BORDERS

8 Position the cursor where you want to turn off the border. Then follow Step 2

9 WordPerfect calls up the Create Paragraph Border, Create Page Border or Create Column Border dialog boxes, according to the border type. Select Off

Tip:

The use of appropriate border and fill styles can enhance documents enormously. For instance, borders around pages make correspondence much more visually effective

Fill Styles dialog box (called up from step 4 on page 89)

```
                          Fill Styles
List Styles From:   ● Document    ○ Personal Library    ○ Shared Library

   [None]                                    1. Select
  •10% Shaded Fill                           2. Create...
  •20% Shaded Fill                           3. Edit...
  •30% Shaded Fill                           4. Delete
  •40% Shaded Fill                           5. Copy...
  •50% Shaded Fill                           6. Save...
  •60% Shaded Fill                           7. Retrieve...
  •70% Shaded Fill                           8. Options...
  •80% Shaded Fill                           N. Name Search

  • Denotes library style

                                                       Close
```

Double-click chosen fill style (7)

91

Summary for Section 5

WordPerfect 6.0 for DOS lets you work with text in a variety of ways:

- You can *block* — or select — text (often a precursor for the actions described below).

- You can apply formatting options.

- You can perform copy, cut and paste operations.

- You can delete text.

- You can undelete text.

- You can specify text alignment.

- You can amend line spacing.

- You can apply automatic hyphenation.

- You can surround text with borders.

6   Document checking

Spell checking

Use WordPerfect's Speller to proof documents.

Speller highlights spelling errors and common typographical mistakes. For instance, duplicated words and lower-case words which contain capital letters (as in *speLler*) are flagged. Speller also highlights instances of numbers within words.

There are four basic options:

● Word — checks the word in which the cursor is located

● Page — checks the page in which the cursor is located

● Document — checks the whole of the current document

● From Cursor — works from the current cursor position and checks the remainder of the document.

1 Position the cursor within a document. Choose **Tools↪Writing Tools**. This calls up the Writing Tools dialog box

2 Select Speller. The Speller dialog box is called up

3 Click Word, Page, Document or From Cursor. Speller stops at the first unknown word it finds and displays the Word Not Found dialog box

4 Refer to the Suggestions field. If one of Speller's alternative suggestions is correct, double-click it or highlight it and select Replace Word

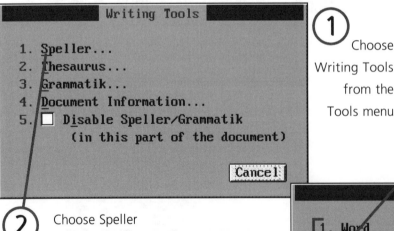

① Choose Writing Tools from the Tools menu

② Choose Speller

③ Click the option you require

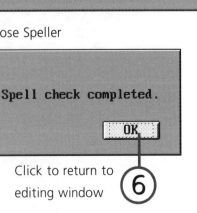

Spell check completed.

OK

Click to return to editing window ⑥

94

5 If none of Speller's suggested replacements are correct, choose Skip Once, Skip in this Document, Add to Dictionary, Edit Word, Lookup or Ignore Numbers

6 When Speller finishes it displays the Spell check completed dialog box. Click OK to return to the editing window

When Speller has highlighted a word it believes to be incorrect, you have several options. Speller normally provides a list of alternative words; you can replace the incorrect word with one of these. Or you can select:

● Skip Once — Speller ignores this instance of the word but flags later occurrences

● Skip in this Document — Speller ignores this and later occurrences

● Add to Dictionary — Speller adds the word to its dictionary

● Edit Word — Speller lets you edit the word. Press [F7] to confirm the alterations and return to Speller

● Lookup — Speller displays a list of phonetic equivalents (e.g. if the flagged word is *farmacy*, Speller suggests *pharmacy*)

● Ignore Numbers — Speller ignores numbers in words.

This is an illustration of Word-Perfect's Speller.
When it encounters a word it doesn't recognise (e.g. 'errer'), Speller produces its Word Not Found dialogue.

If a word is not recognised, it is placed in the Word entry box

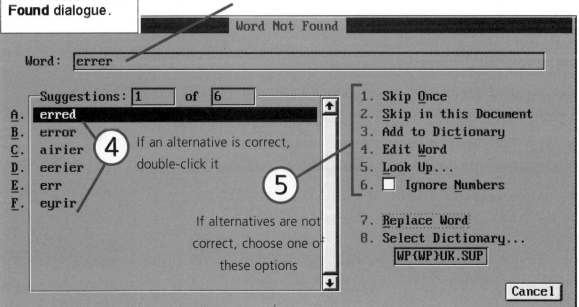

Word Not Found

Word: errer

Suggestions: 1 of 6

A. erred
B. error
C. airier
D. eerier
E. err
F. eyrir

④ If an alternative is correct, double-click it

⑤

If alternatives are not correct, choose one of these options

1. Skip Once
2. Skip in this Document
3. Add to Dictionary
4. Edit Word
5. Look Up...
6. ☐ Ignore Numbers

7. Replace Word
8. Select Dictionary...
   WP{WP}UK.SUP

Cancel

The Thesaurus

Use WordPerfect's in-built Thesaurus to find synonyms for words.

You can also use the Thesaurus to produce antonyms.

Initially, the Thesaurus lists alternatives in a column on the left of the screen. Entries are categorised:

- (n)   nouns
- (v)   verbs
- (a)   adjectives
- (ant)   antonyms.

Words marked with the symbol · can also be looked up. When you do so, a new column of suggestions is opened to the right of the original. You can have up to three columns at once.

Once you've found your *mot juste* you can prompt the Thesaurus to substitute it for the original word.

The following options are available from the Thesaurus dialog box:

● Look Up — use this to look up non-related words from within the Thesaurus itself. Select Look Up. Type in the word in the Word field and press Enter.

● View — displays the current document above the Thesaurus. Press F7 to return to the Thesaurus.

● Clear Column — moves columns of alternatives to the left. Use this if too many columns are displayed.

● History — shows a list of the words you've looked up so far in the current Thesaurus session.

1 Position the cursor in the word you want alternatives for, then choose **Tools→Writing Tools**. This calls up the Writing Tools dialog box (we saw this already, on page 94)

2 Click Thesaurus

3 If you need further, related suggestions, double-click on any word prefaced with the symbol ·. WordPerfect opens an additional column

4 To replace your original word with the new word, highlight the replacement and click Replace

5 If you decide not to replace the original word, click Cancel to return to the document window

① Choose Writing Tools from the Tools menu

② Click to call up WordPerfect's Thesaurus

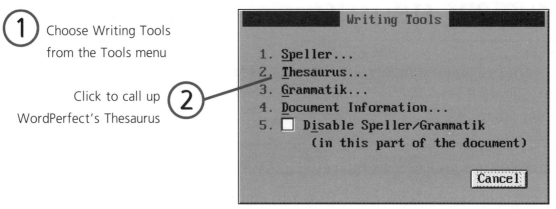

Writing Tools

1. Speller...
2. Thesaurus...
3. Grammatik...
4. Document Information...
5. ☐ Disable Speller/Grammatik
   (in this part of the document)

Cancel

Expressions with a • symbol in front have further related expressions. Double-click to launch additional columns ③

The Thesaurus contains up to three columns of related expressions.

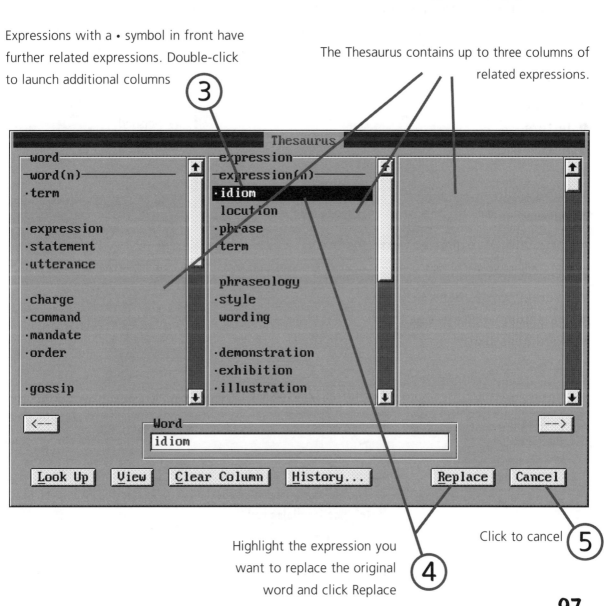

Thesaurus

word
word(n)
·term

·expression
·statement
·utterance

·charge
·command
·mandate
·order

·gossip

expression
expression(n)
·**idiom**
locution
·phrase
·term

phraseology
·style
wording

·demonstration
·exhibition
·illustration

Word
idiom

Look Up   View   Clear Column   History...   Replace   Cancel

Highlight the expression you want to replace the original word and click Replace ④

Click to cancel ⑤

97

Document statistics

Most word processors supply a word–count feature because knowing how many words are in a document is often important.

Writers, particularly, benefit from this: they frequently have to write to wordage restrictions.

WordPerfect 6, however, provides access to a host of further, related statistics which can be useful when it comes to assessing the overall impact of a document. When you tell WordPerfect to determine the word count, it also calculates the number of:

- characters
- letters
- lines
- sentences
- paragraphs
- pages.

Additionally, WordPerfect establishes:

- average word length
- average words per sentence
- maximum words per sentence
- document size.

1 From within the document whose statistics you need, choose **Tools ↳ Writing Tools**. This calls up the Writing Tools dialog box, as on the previous pages

2 Click on Document Information. This calls up the Document Information dialog box

3 Click OK when you've finished

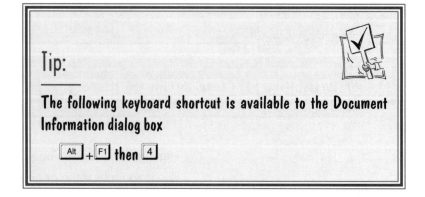

Tip:

The following keyboard shortcut is available to the Document Information dialog box

Alt + F1 **then** 4

98

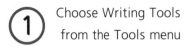

① Choose Writing Tools
from the Tools menu

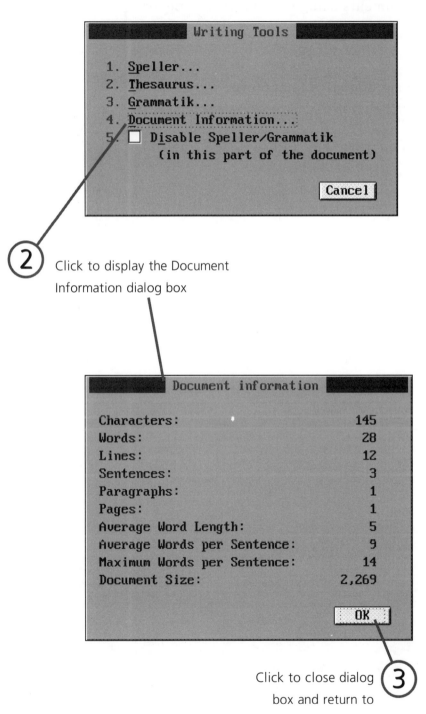

Writing Tools

1. Speller...
2. Thesaurus...
3. Grammatik...
4. Document Information...
5. ☐ Disable Speller/Grammatik
   (in this part of the document)

Cancel

② Click to display the Document
Information dialog box

Document information

Characters:	145
Words:	28
Lines:	12
Sentences:	3
Paragraphs:	1
Pages:	1
Average Word Length:	5
Average Words per Sentence:	9
Maximum Words per Sentence:	14
Document Size:	2,269

OK

③ Click to close dialog
box and return to
editing window

Summary for Section 6

- Spell check documents using WordPerfect's Speller.

- Use the Thesaurus to find alternatives for overused words.

- Invoke Document Statistics to achieve:

  ❑ a word count

  ❑ information on word, line and sentence length.

7 Page layout

Paper sizes

WordPerfect 6 comes with a variety of pre-defined paper sizes (or *definitions*).

The range available to you depends on the printer currently selected (see page 140 for information on how to select printers). However, you can amend existing paper definitions or create your own.

When you select a paper size, WordPerfect uses this information to format and print your documents accurately. You can apply new paper definitions to all or part of a current document.

SELECTING EXISTING PAPER TYPE

1 Position the cursor on the page from which you want the new paper size to apply. Then choose **Layout⤷Page** to call up the Page Format dialog box

2 Click Paper Size/Type. This calls up the Paper Size/ Type dialog box

① Choose Page from the Layout menu

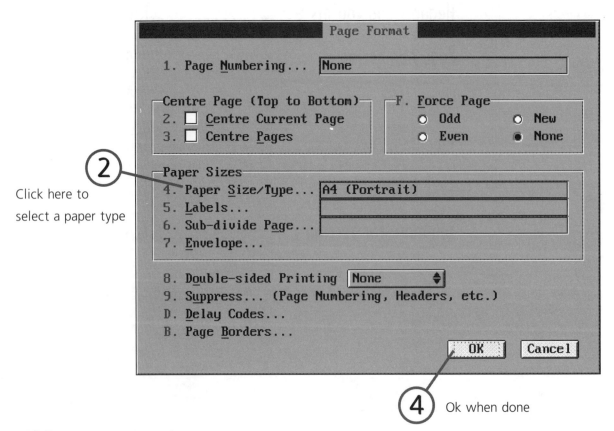

Click here to select a paper type

②

④ Ok when done

102

3 Double–click the correct paper definition (or highlight it and click Select).

4 In the Page Format dialog box, click OK to confirm

WordPerfect's paper sizes don't just contain information relating to the physical measurements of the page. For instance, if a document contains more than one paper size, you can modify the relevant paper definitions so that WordPerfect will prompt you when the paper in the printer needs changing.

Double-click the correct definition ③

⑤ Choose edit to amend existing paper types

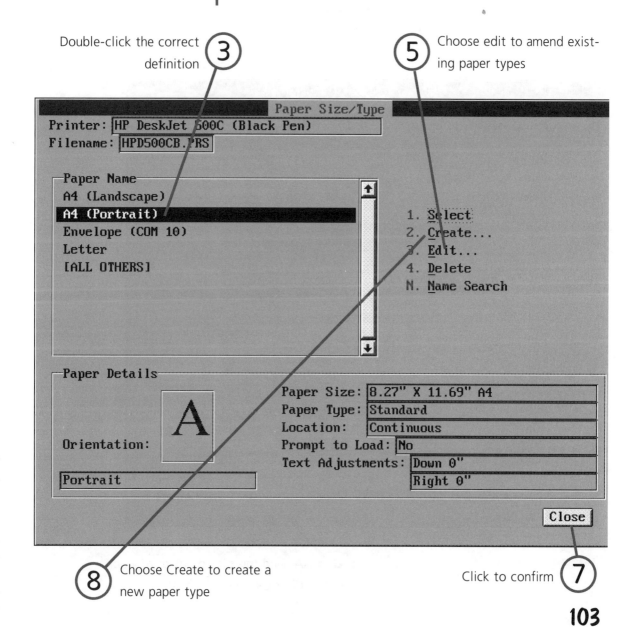

Paper Size/Type

Printer: HP DeskJet 500C (Black Pen)
Filename: HPD500CB.PRS

Paper Name
A4 (Landscape)
A4 (Portrait)
Envelope (COM 10)
Letter
[ALL OTHERS]

1. Select
2. Create...
3. Edit...
4. Delete
N. Name Search

Paper Details

A

Orientation:

Portrait

Paper Size: 8.27" X 11.69" A4
Paper Type: Standard
Location: Continuous
Prompt to Load: No
Text Adjustments: Down 0"
                  Right 0"

Close

⑧ Choose Create to create a new paper type

Click to confirm ⑦

103

Paper sizes (contd)

5 Follow Steps 1 and 2. Then highlight the paper type you want to change and select Edit. This calls up the Edit Paper Size/Type dialog box

6 Make the appropriate amendments and click OK to confirm.

7 In the Paper Size/Type dialog box, click Close

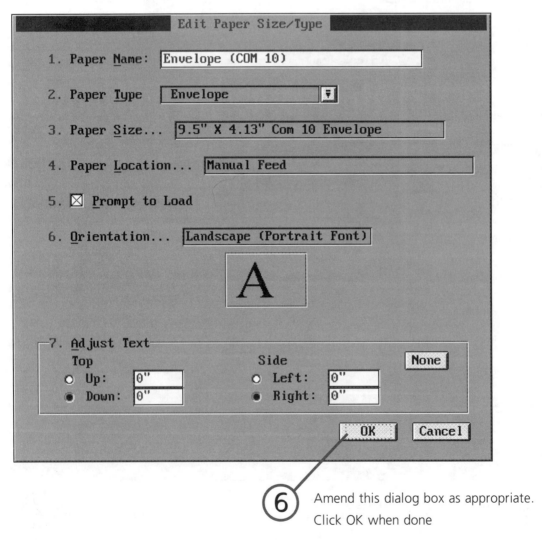

Amend this dialog box as appropriate. Click OK when done

CREATING A NEW PAPER TYPE

8 Follow Steps 1 and 2. Then highlight the existing paper type which is nearest to the one you want to establish and select Create. This calls up the Create Paper Size/Type dialog box

9 Enter a name for the new paper type, then make any appropriate amendments. Click OK followed by Close in the Paper Size/ Type dialog box to confirm

```
┌────────────────────────────────────────────────┐
│              Create Paper Size/Type             │
│                                                 │
│  Paper Name:  │New                            │ │
│                                                 │
│  Paper Type   │ Envelope            │ ▼ │       │
│                                                 │
│  Paper Size...  │9.5" X 4.13" Com 10 Envelope │ │
│                                                 │
│  Paper Location...  │Manual Feed              │ │
│                                                 │
│  ⊠ Prompt to Load                               │
│                                                 │
│  Orientation...  │Landscape (Portrait Font)│    │
│                                                 │
│                 ┌─────────┐                     │
│                 │         │                     │
│                 │    A    │                     │
│                 │         │                     │
│                 └─────────┘                     │
│                                                 │
│  ┌─Adjust Text──────────────────────────┐       │
│  │ Top                  Side    ┌──────┐ │       │
│  │ ○ Up:  │0"│      ○ Left:  │0"│ None │ │       │
│  │ ○ Down:│0"│      ○ Right: │0"│└──────┘ │      │
│  └──────────────────────────────────────┘       │
│                         ┌────OK────┐ ┌─Cancel─┐  │
│                         └──────────┘ └────────┘  │
└────────────────────────────────────────────────┘
```

9

Amend this dialog box as appropriate.
Click OK when done

Margins

WordPerfect 6 lets you adjust document and paragraph margins.

Document margins are the left, right, top and bottom page margins; WordPerfect defaults to settings of 1 inch for each. Paragraph margins are left and right margins applying either to specified paragraphs, or onwards from the position of the cursor. Paragraph margins also include subsidiary features:

- First Line Indent — indents the first line of each paragraph automatically by the amount specified.
- Paragraph Spacing — inserts a specified gap between paragraphs whenever you press Return.

You can insert minus numbers as paragraph margins, but not as document margins. As an illustration, blocking a paragraph and entering a negative first line indent reverses the normal indent direction i.e. the first line is 'outdented' to the left of the rest of the paragraph.

Basic steps:

DOCUMENT MARGINS

1 Position the cursor at the point from which you need to amend the margins, then choose **Layout↳Margins**. This calls up the Margin Format dialog box

2 Amend the Left, Right, Top and Bottom margins as appropriate. Click OK when you've finished

PARAGRAPH MARGINS

3 Block the relevant paragraph(s). Or position the cursor at the point from which you need the revised Paragraph margins to apply. Now follow Step 1

4 Make the necessary adjustments and click OK when you've finished

Tip:

If you want to set revised margins for all documents, use the Document Initial Codes feature (see page 33)

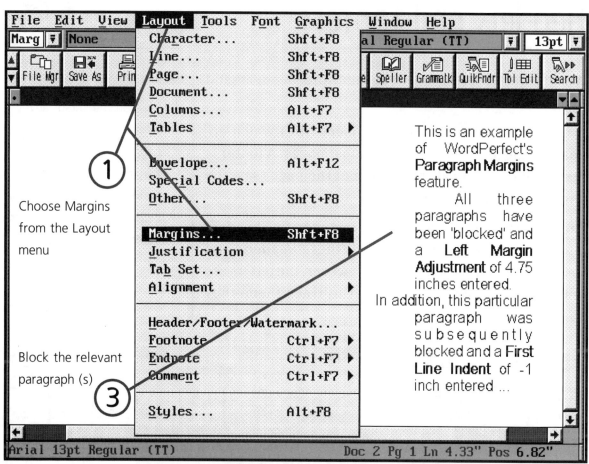

Choose Margins from the Layout menu

Block the relevant paragraph (s)

This is an example of WordPerfect's **Paragraph Margins** feature.

All three paragraphs have been 'blocked' and a **Left Margin Adjustment** of 4.75 inches entered. In addition, this particular paragraph was subsequently blocked and a **First Line Indent** of -1 inch entered ...

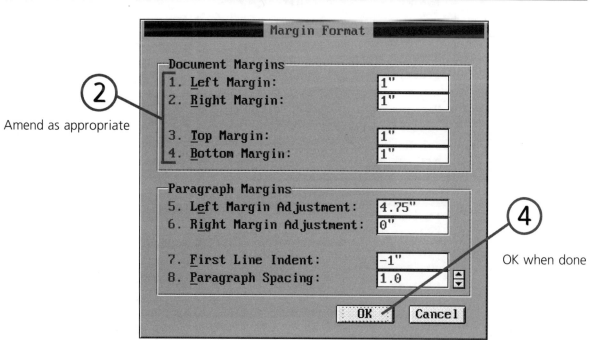

Amend as appropriate

OK when done

Headers and footers

WordPerfect 6 lets you have multiple headers and footers within documents.

A header is text (often the document title) which appears at the top of each page, or most pages. A footer is text which appears at the bottom of the page (say, the page number).

Each page in WordPerfect 6 can have up to two headers and two footers. WordPerfect calls these *Header A* and *Header B, Footer A* and *Footer B.* However, the letters are only there to enable WordPerfect to track them: they have no other significance.

CREATING A HEADER OR FOOTER

1 Position the cursor anywhere on the relevant page. Choose **Layout⤷Header/ Footer/Watermark**. This calls up the Header/Footer/ Watermark dialog box

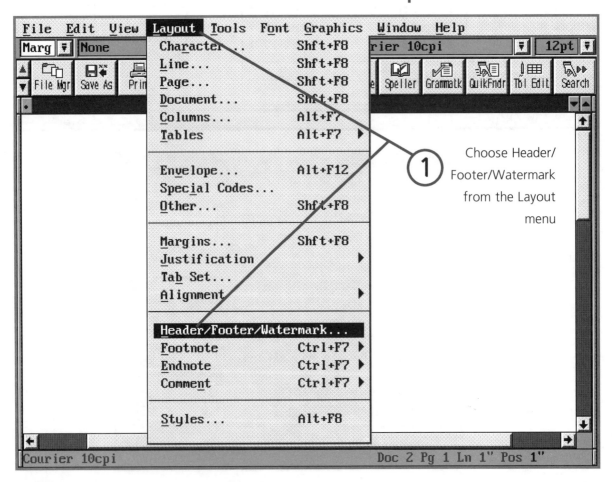

Choose Header/ Footer/Watermark from the Layout menu

2 Click Header A or Header B, or Footer A or Footer B, as appropriate, to call up the respective header or footer dialog box. Select OK when done

3 Select All Pages to have the header or footer apply to the entire document. Select Even Pages or Odd Pages to limit the header or footer to even or odd pages only

4 Click Create

5 WordPerfect launches its special header/footer editor (see over). Enter the relevant text. Apply any formatting (e.g. font attributes) you need. Or refer to page 114 if you want to insert automatic page numbers

6 Press F7 to return to the document

There are two ways to view headers and footers on screen. Switch to Page mode (see page 16) or use Print Preview (see page 138).

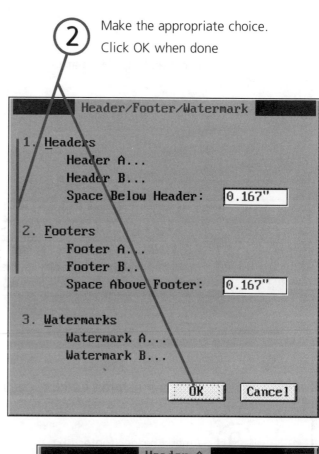

2 — Make the appropriate choice. Click OK when done

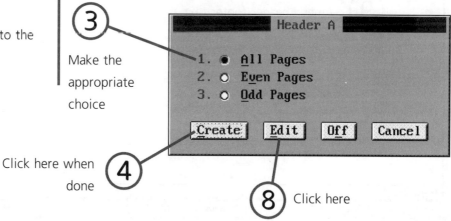

3 — Make the appropriate choice

Click here when done — 4

8 — Click here

Headers & footers (contd)

7 Follow Steps 1, 2 and 3 on previous pages

8 Click Edit, to call up the editor

9 Amend the header/footer text

10 Press F7 when you've finished

(5) Enter text and apply formatting...

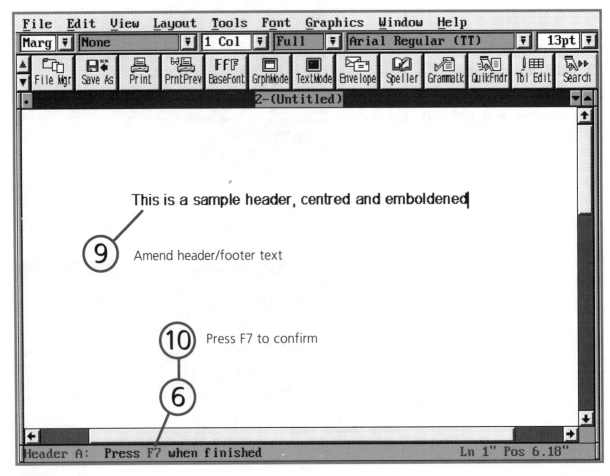

This is a sample header, centred and emboldened

(9) Amend header/footer text

(10) Press F7 to confirm

(6)

Header A: Press F7 when finished   Ln 1" Pos 6.18"

SUPPRESSING HEADERS OR FOOTERS

1 Position the cursor on the page whose header and/or footer you want to disable. Now choose **Layout↳Page**, to call up the Page Format dialog box

2 Click Suppress, which calls up the Suppress (This Page Only) dialog box (see over)

You may not wish headers and footers you've created to appear on every page of a document.

For instance, many documents where the header incorporates the title do not require the header to be printed on page 1: the title is already there. WordPerfect 6 calls this *suppressing* a header or footer. When you suppress a header or footer, the effect is limited to the page in which the cursor is currently situated. Headers and footers on earlier and subsequent pages are unaffected.

On the other hand, turning off headers or footers disables them from that point onwards.

① Choose Page from the Layout menu

② Choose Suppress

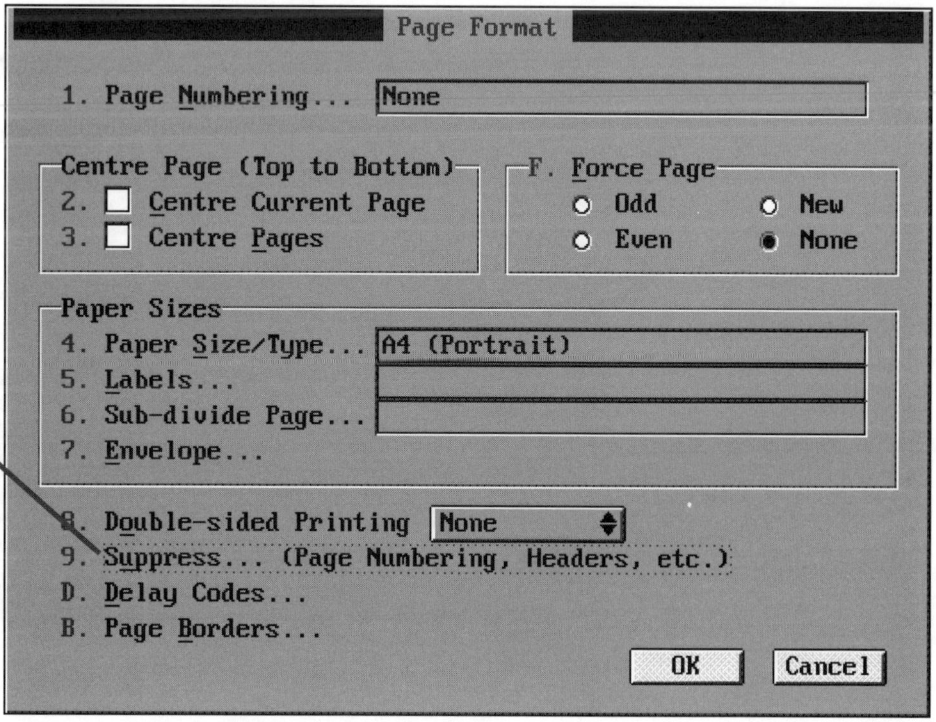

Headers & footers (contd)

Basic steps:

3 Select the items you wish
  suppressed. Then click OK

TURNING OFF HEADERS OR
     FOOTERS

4 Position the cursor on the
  first page whose header
  and/or footer you wish to
  disable (WordPerfect will
  turn off this feature for
  subsequent pages, too).

Tip:

Another way to remove a header or footer is to use WordPerfect's
Reveal Codes feature (see page 31) to display the formatting
code. Once displayed, it can be highlighted with the cursor and
deleted with the [Delete] or [Back space] keys

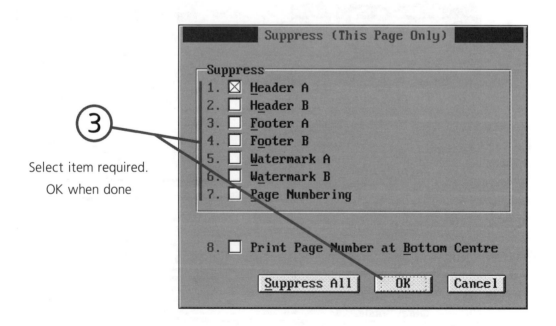

Select item required.
OK when done

③

Suppress (This Page Only)
Suppress
1. ☒ Header A
2. ☐ Header B
3. ☐ Footer A
4. ☐ Footer B
5. ☐ Watermark A
6. ☐ Watermark B
7. ☐ Page Numbering
8. ☐ Print Page Number at Bottom Centre
Suppress All   OK   Cancel

Now choose
**Layout↳Header/
Footer/Watermark**, to
call up the Header/Footer/
Watermark dialog box

5 Select the relevant header
or footer, to call up its
dialog box

6 Click Off

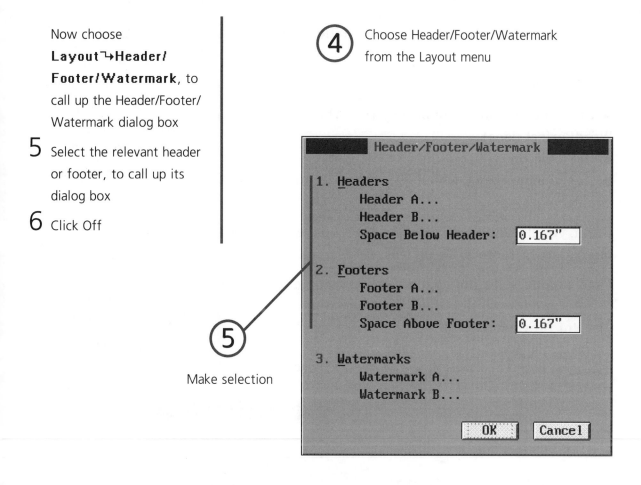

④ Choose Header/Footer/Watermark
from the Layout menu

⑤ Make selection

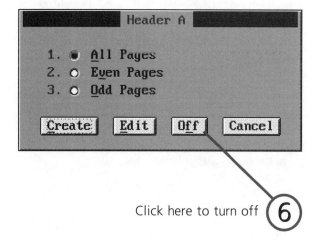

Click here to turn off ⑥

Page numbering

If you wish, WordPerfect 6 will automatically number pages for you.

You can specify:

● the type of page numbering (i.e. the characters WordPerfect uses)
● the location
● the number from which WordPerfect begins the count.

Often, you'll want WordPerfect to insert page numbers in headers or footers. To do this, refer to page 108.

Page numbers do not display on screen in Text or Graphic modes. To view them, use Page Mode (page 16) or Print Preview (page 138).

INSERTING PAGE NUMBERS

1 Position the cursor on the page from which you want automatic numbering to start. Then choose **Layout‶Page**. This calls up the Page Format dialog box

2 Click Page Numbering. This calls up the Page Numbering dialog box

3 Click Page Number Position. This calls up the Page Number Position dialog box

① Choose Page from the Layout menu

```
                        Page Format

  1. Page Numbering...  None

  ┌Centre Page (Top to Bottom)┐  ┌F. Force Page──────────┐
  2. ☐ Centre Current Page       │  ○ Odd      ○ New
  3. ☐ Centre Pages              │  ○ Even     ● None

  ┌Paper Sizes──────────────────────────────────────┐
  4. Paper Size/Type...  A4 (Portrait)
  5. Labels...
  6. Sub-divide Page...
  7. Envelope...

  8. Double-sided Printing  None        ▲▼
  9. Suppress... (Page Numbering, Headers, etc.)
  D. Delay Codes...
  B. Page Borders...
                                      │  OK  │  Cancel  │
```

② Click here to call up Page Numbering dialog box

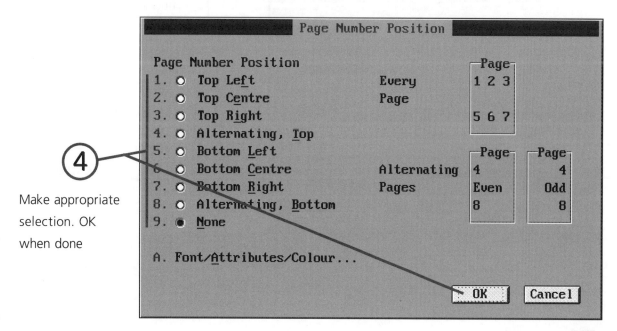

4 Select the appropriate
position. Click OK when
you've finished

③ Click here to call up Page Numbering
Position dialog box

Page Numbering

1. Page Number Position... [None]

2. Page Number... [1]

3. Secondary Page Number... [1]

4. Chapter... [1]

5. Volume... [1]

6. Page Number Format [page num]

7. Insert Formatted Page Number

[Number Codes... F5]   [OK]   [Cancel]

Page Number Position

Page Number Position

			Page	
1. ○ Top Left	Every		1 2 3	
2. ○ Top Centre	Page			
3. ○ Top Right			5 6 7	
4. ○ Alternating, Top				
5. ○ Bottom Left			Page	Page
6. ○ Bottom Centre	Alternating		4	4
7. ○ Bottom Right	Pages		Even	Odd
8. ○ Alternating, Bottom			8	8
9. ● None				

A. Font/Attributes/Colour...

[OK]   [Cancel]

④ Make appropriate
selection. OK
when done

115

Page numbering (contd)

Tip:

Varying the numbering method can make long documents look more effective. For example, in a Preface use Lower Roman...

5 Place the cursor on the page on which you wish the amendments to begin. Now follow Steps 1 and 2, and click Page Number to call up the Set Page Number dialog box. To make WordPerfect count from a number other than 1, enter the required number

6 To change the character WordPerfect uses, click Numbering Method. Make the appropriate selection from the drop–down list. Click OK when you've finished

⑤ Enter required number here

Set Page Number

New Number: | 1

Numbering Method | ▸Numbers
Lower Letters
☐ Increment Number | Upper Letters
Lower Roman
☐ Decrement Number | Upper Roman

☐ Display in Document

OK ◂ | Cancel

⑥

Click here and make appropriate selection from list. OK when done

Using tabs

Tabs are one means of indenting text.

Strictly speaking, *indenting* refers to any variation in line length. However, a more specific definition is: moving a line of text by a specific amount (usually in from the left margin). To do this, WordPerfect provides a series of preset tab stops to which the text can be moved successively.

You can amend these tab stops as necessary.

Use tabs to indent single lines of text, or the first lines of paragraphs.

Basic steps:

INSERTING TABS

1 To move a line one tab stop to the right, place the cursor at the start of the relevant line and press `Tab`

2 To move a line one tab stop to the left, place the cursor at the start of the line and press `Shift` + `Tab`

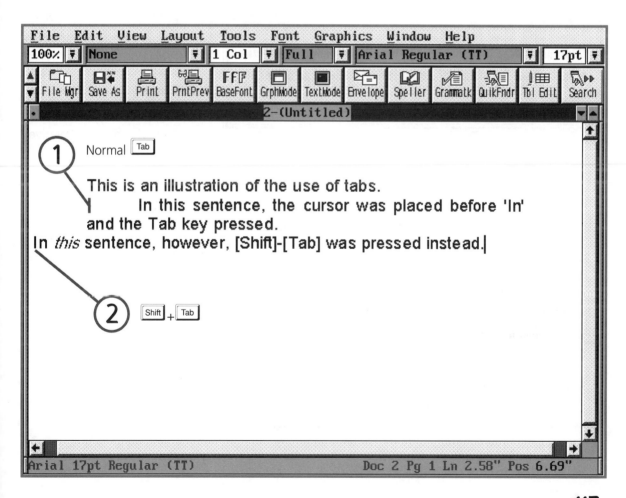

Using tabs (contd)

There are two kinds of tabs in WordPerfect 6:

● relative — measured from the text margins. Changes to margins are reflected in the tabs.

● absolute — measured from the left page edge. Do not vary.

Tip:

Don't use spaces to move text in at the start of paragraphs – use tabs, instead. Amending tabs later is a lot easier than amending spaces

Take note:

Don't confuse tabs with WordPerfect's Indent feature (see page 120). Indenting moves whole paragraphs, not just the first line, in from the margin.

Don't use tabs to tabulate large sections of text; use WordPerfect's Column feature (see page 122) instead

AMENDING TAB SETTINGS

1 Place the cursor at the point from which you wish the amendments to take effect. Now choose **Layout ⤷ Tab Set**. This calls up the Tab Set dialog box

2 To delete all existing tab stops, select Clear All. To delete a specific tab stop, press ⌊Tab⌋ until the cursor is over the stop. Then click Clear One (or press ⌊Delete⌋)

3 Before you insert new tab stops, first specify the type of tab. Click Relative or Absolute

4 To insert a series of uniform tab stops, type a figure in Repeat Every. For instance, if you type in 0.75", WordPerfect inserts tab stops at $3/_4$ inch intervals

5 To insert a specific tab stop, double–click on the correct location within the ruler

6 Click OK when you've finished

(1) Choose Tab Set from the Layout menu

(5) Double-click anywhere here to insert a specific tab stop

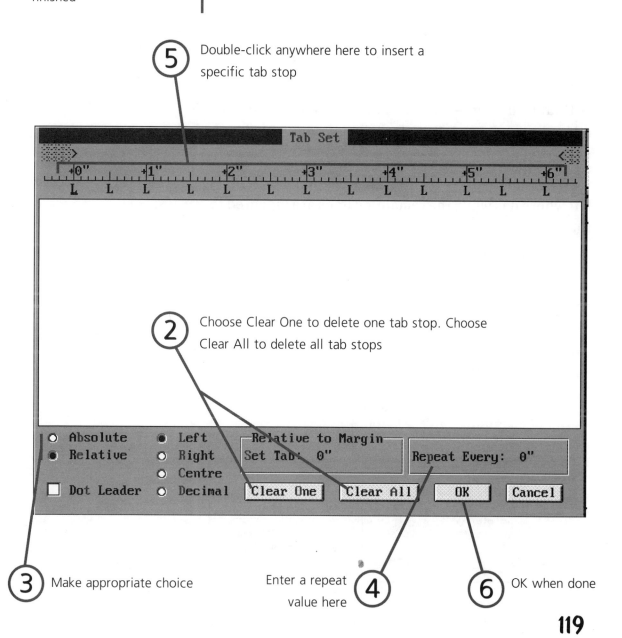

(2) Choose Clear One to delete one tab stop. Choose Clear All to delete all tab stops

(3) Make appropriate choice

Enter a repeat value here (4)

(6) OK when done

Indents

WordPerfect 6's indents are specialised tabs. In other programs, they're sometimes known as *hard tabs.*

The difference is this. Whereas tabs move *single lines* of text to the next or preceding tab stop (see page 117 for information on tab settings), indents move whole *paragraphs.*

The following options are available:

● Indent — moves a paragraph to the next tab stop to the right of the left margin.

● Double–indent — the paragraph is moved in by one tab stop from the left AND right margins simultaneously.

● Hanging Indent — the first line of the paragraph is left where it is while the remaining lines are indented to the right.

APPLYING INDENTS BEFORE YOU
ENTER TEXT

1 Choose
Layout⮬Alignment.
From the sub-menu choose
Indent o, Indent on or
Hanging Indent

2 Begin to enter text. Press
⏎ to end the indentation

APPLYING INDENTS TO EXISTING
TEXT

3 Position the cursor at the
start of the relevant
paragraph. Then follow
Step 1

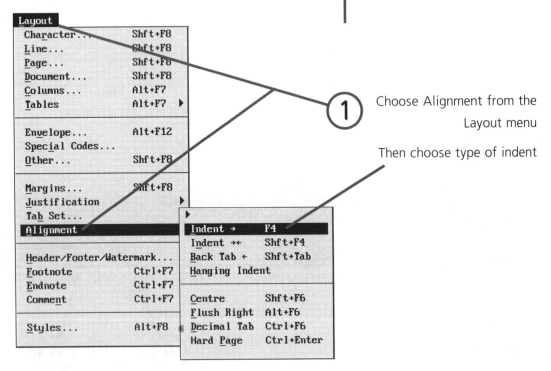

1 Choose Alignment from the
Layout menu

Then choose type of indent

120

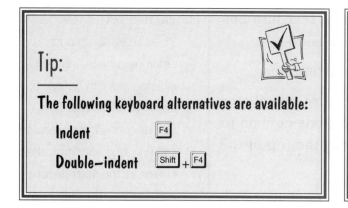
 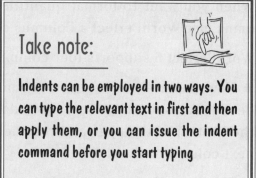
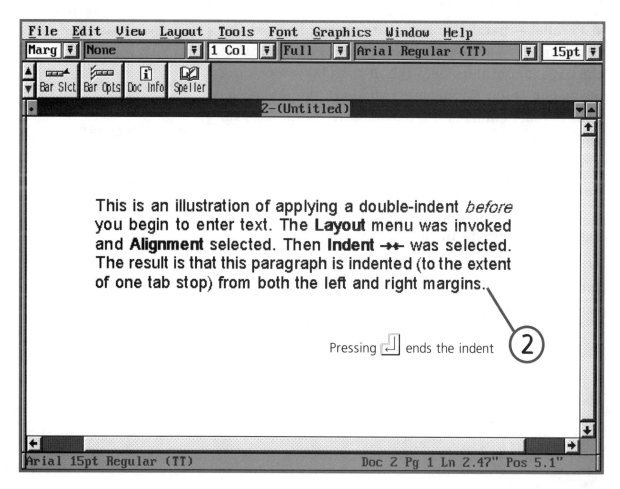

File Edit View Layout Tools Font Graphics Window Help

Marg ▼ None ▼ 1 Col ▼ Full ▼ Arial Regular (TT) ▼ 15pt ▼

Bar Slct Bar Opts Doc Info Speller

2-(Untitled)

This is an illustration of applying a double-indent *before* you begin to enter text. The **Layout** menu was invoked and **Alignment** selected. Then **Indent** →⊦ was selected. The result is that this paragraph is indented (to the extent of one tab stop) from both the left and right margins.

Pressing ⏎ ends the indent ②

Arial 15pt Regular (TT)   Doc 2 Pg 1 Ln 2.47" Pos 5.1"

Text columns

When you want to format quantities of text into columns, use WordPerfect's Columns command.

WordPerfect 6 supports four column definitions:

● Newspaper — newspaper columns are sometimes described as *snaking*. Text flows down one column to the bottom of the page and resumes at the top of the next column to the right.

● Balanced Newspaper — balanced newspaper columns form a special case. With balanced newspaper columns, WordPerfect ensures that each snaking column is identical in length.

● Parallel — parallel columns are grouped across the page in rows. When each column reaches the bottom of the page it continues onto the next. Subsequent rows are begun below the longest column in the preceding row. Parallel columns are particularly useful for lists and scripts.

● Parallel with Block Protect — parallel columns with one difference. If one column in a horizontal row extends onto a new page, WordPerfect ensures that the entire row moves to the new page.

WordPerfect 6 lets you specify the number of columns, the gap between columns and the distance between each horizontal row.

Basic steps:

FORMATTING TEXT INTO COLUMNS
   You can either impose columns on existing text, or impose them before you begin to enter text (if you're applying columns to existing text, position the cursor at the start before carrying out the following Steps).

1 Choose **Layout↪Columns**. This calls up the Text Columns dialog box

2 Make the appropriate selections. Click OK when finished

TURNING OFF COLUMNS

3 Position the cursor within the column. Then follow Step 1

4 Click Off

Tip:

When within a column, press `Ctrl`+`⏎` to begin a new column

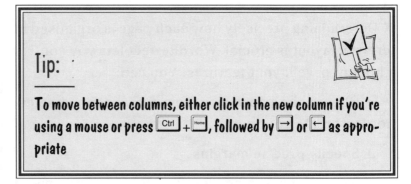

Tip:

To move between columns, either click in the new column if you're using a mouse or press `Ctrl`+`Home`, followed by `→` or `←` as appropriate

① Choose Columns from the Layout menu

②

Choose the column type. OK when done

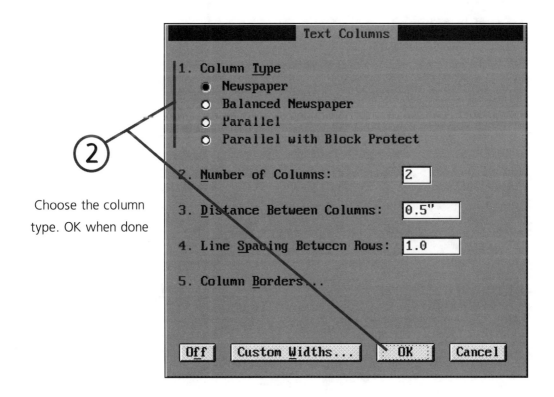

Summary for Section 7

● Determining precisely how each page is organised in terms of layout is crucial. WordPerfect lets you control a host of page layout features. You can:

❑ Choose the paper size from a pre–defined selection, or create your own.

❑ Specify precise margins.

❑ Set up your own headers and footers, and amend them if you need to.

❑ Turn off headers and footers on a page-by-page basis.

❑ Implement automatic page numbering.

❑ Apply tabs and indents.

❑ Organise text in columns.

8   Styles

Creating styles

In WordPerfect 6, *styles* are collections of formatting commands.

The usefulness of styles lies in the fact that the associated commands can be imposed *en bloc*, a great time-saving feature. A useful corollary is that you can amend individual formatting features just as easily.

Here's an example. Suppose you're working on a fairly long document which contains body text, headings and sub–headings. The body text (the bulk of the document) is in Courier, a typeface which resembles typewriter output, while the headings and sub-headings which interrupt it periodically are in different faces. If, say, you wanted to change the body text to Times New Roman, you'd normally have to go through the document, manually changing each section and carefully skipping each heading and sub-heading. This is a time-consuming process. However, if you've defined a style for the body text, you can simply make one small change to the style. WordPerfect will then automatically update all text linked to the style.

WordPerfect has three kinds of style:

● paragraph — applies to paragraphs containing the cursor or to blocked text
● character — applies to text you're about to type in or to blocked text
● open — applies to all text after the cursor.

Paragraph styles are most suitable for headings, character styles for single words or brief phrases.

1 Position the cursor in the relevant text, or block it first. Now choose **Layout↳Styles**. This calls up the Style List dialog box

2 Click Create. This calls up the Create Style dialog box

3 Enter a name for the new style

4 Click Style Type and select the appropriate style definition from the drop-down list

5 If you've selected Paragraph Style or Character Style and want the new style to adopt the attributes of the text which is currently blocked (or in which the cursor is currently located), select Create from Current Paragraph or Create from Current Character (WordPerfect varies the wording accordingly). The Edit Style dialog box (over) is called up, which shows the style contents

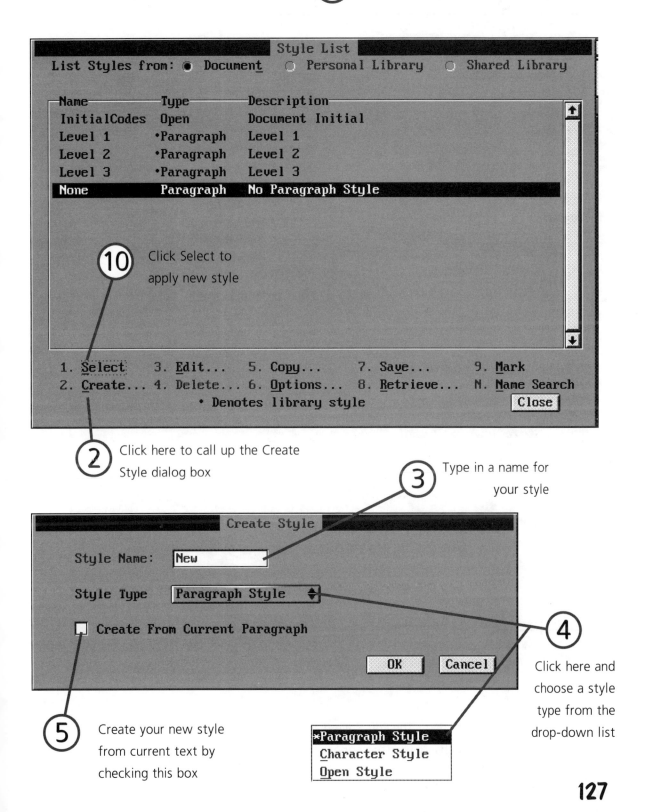

① Choose Styles from the Layout menu

Style List

List Styles from: ● Document   ○ Personal Library   ○ Shared Library

Name	Type	Description
InitialCodes	Open	Document Initial
Level 1	•Paragraph	Level 1
Level 2	•Paragraph	Level 2
Level 3	•Paragraph	Level 3
None	**Paragraph**	**No Paragraph Style**

⑩ Click Select to apply new style

1. Select   3. Edit...   5. Copy...   7. Save...   9. Mark
2. Create... 4. Delete... 6. Options... 8. Retrieve... N. Name Search
              • Denotes library style   Close

② Click here to call up the Create Style dialog box

③ Type in a name for your style

Create Style

Style Name: New

Style Type   Paragraph Style ⬍

☐ Create From Current Paragraph

                        OK   Cancel

④ Click here and choose a style type from the drop-down list

⑤ Create your new style from current text by checking this box

*Paragraph Style
 Character Style
 Open Style

127

Creating styles (contd)

Take note:

Choosing Style Contents changes the Edit Style dialog box

6 Enter a description (optional)

7 Choose Style Contents. Now define the style attributes by pulling down the appropriate menu and making your selections. For instance, to have the style italicise all associated text choose **Font⤵Italics**

⑥ Enter description here

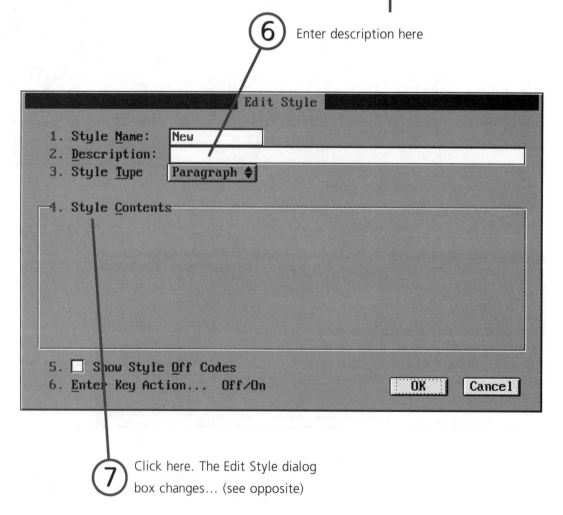

Edit Style

1. Style **N**ame: New
2. **D**escription:
3. Style **T**ype   Paragraph ⬍

4. Style **C**ontents

5. ☐ S**h**ow Style **O**ff Codes
6. **E**nter Key Action...   Off/On   OK   Cancel

⑦ Click here. The Edit Style dialog box changes... (see opposite)

128

8 Press ⌨F7⌨ when you've finished

9 Click OK. You return to the Style List dialog box

10 To apply the new style to the relevant text, ensure it is highlighted and click Select

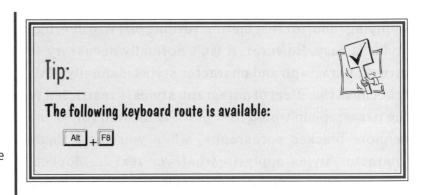

Tip:

The following keyboard route is available:

⌨Alt⌨ + ⌨F8⌨

Relevant formatting controls are shown at the top of the dialog box. As you enter them, formats are listed in the Style Contents area

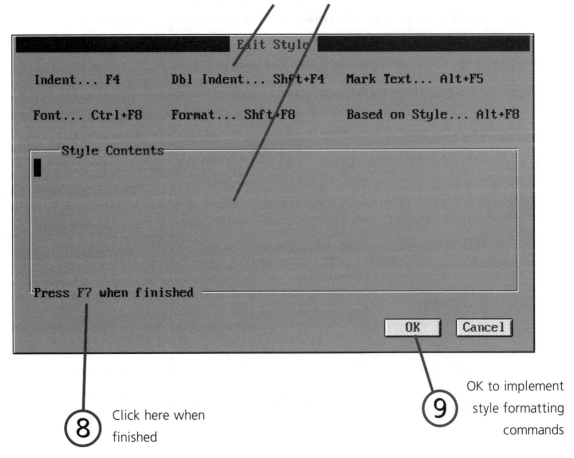

Click here when finished

⑧

OK to implement style formatting commands

⑨

Applying styles

Applying (and, for that matter, turning off) WordPerfect styles is easy. However, it isn't normally necessary to turn off paragraph and character styles manually. This is because the effect of paragraph styles is restricted to the paragraph in which the cursor is located (or to one or more blocked paragraphs) when you apply them. Character styles apply to whatever text is blocked. Consequently, both of these style types turn themselves off automatically.

On the other hand, it is sometimes helpful to deactivate them yourself. For instance, if you've applied a character style to the whole of one line and then decide to limit it to the first two words, you can simply turn the style off after the second word. However, note that if you try this with paragraph styles WordPerfect removes the style entirely from the relevant paragraph.

Open styles, on the other hand, apply to all text following the location of the cursor, and as such can't be turned off. You can, however, use WordPerfect's Reveal Codes feature to delete the appropriate style formatting code (see page 31).

APPLYING STYLES

1 To apply a paragraph style, first position the cursor anywhere within the paragraph (or block all of it). For character styles, block the relevant text. For open styles, simply position the cursor at the point from which you wish the style to apply. Then choose **Layout⤷Styles**, to call up the Style List dialog box

2 Double-click the style (or highlight it and choose Select)

TURNING OFF PARAGRAPH STYLES

3 Position the cursor within the paragraph and follow Step 1, then double-click None (or highlight it and choose Select)

TURNING OFF CHARACTER STYLES

4 Position the cursor at the point from which you want the style to be deactivated and follow Step 1 then click Off

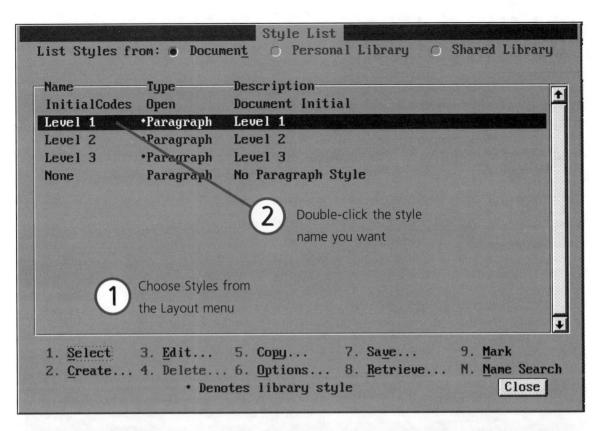

Style List

List Styles from: ● Document   ○ Personal Library   ○ Shared Library

Name	Type	Description
InitialCodes	Open	Document Initial
Level 1	•Paragraph	**Level 1**
Level 2	•Paragraph	Level 2
Level 3	•Paragraph	Level 3
None	Paragraph	No Paragraph Style

② Double-click the style name you want

① Choose Styles from the Layout menu

1. Select   3. Edit...   5. Copy...   7. Save...   9. Mark
2. Create... 4. Delete... 6. Options... 8. Retrieve... N. Name Search
• Denotes library style   Close

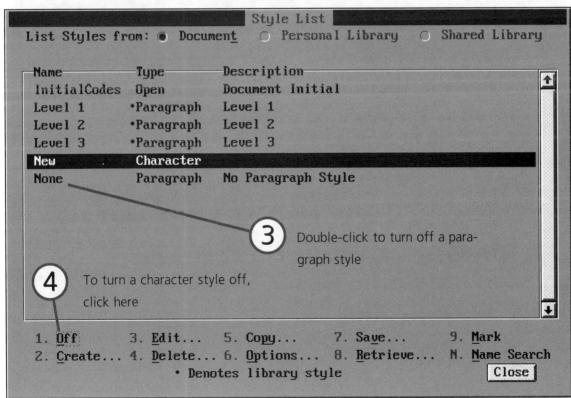

Style List

List Styles from: ● Document   ○ Personal Library   ○ Shared Library

Name	Type	Description
InitialCodes	Open	Document Initial
Level 1	•Paragraph	Level 1
Level 2	•Paragraph	Level 2
Level 3	•Paragraph	Level 3
New	**Character**	
None	Paragraph	No Paragraph Style

③ Double-click to turn off a paragraph style

④ To turn a character style off, click here

1. Off   3. Edit...   5. Copy...   7. Save...   9. Mark
2. Create... 4. Delete... 6. Options... 8. Retrieve... N. Name Search
• Denotes library style   Close

Modifying styles

Styles you've set up — or existing styles provided by WordPerfect — can be modified very easily.

WordPerfect's use of formatting codes within styles makes it simple to see exactly what attributes a style contains. You can delete inappropriate codes directly, or pull down WordPerfect's menus and implement new commands.

Any changes you make to styles are applied to the whole document.

Basic steps:

1 Choose
   Layout↳Styles, to call
   up the Style List dialog box

2 Highlight the style you
   want to amend and click
   Edit. This calls up the Edit
   Style dialog box

① Choose Styles from the Layout menu

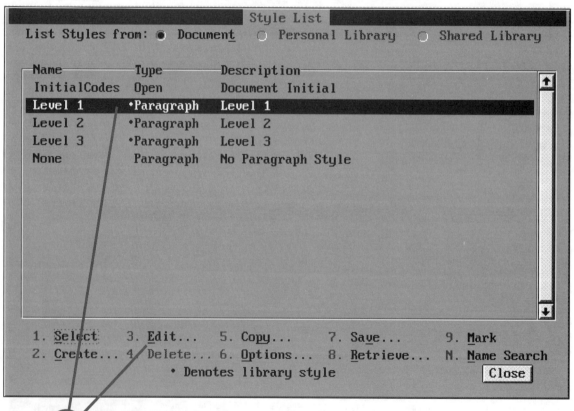

② Select the style you want to
modify, then click Edit

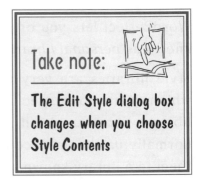

3 Select Style Contents. Choose your required new options from the various menus. To delete unwanted formatting codes, highlight them and press [Delete]

4 Press [F7] when you've finished

Take note:

The Edit Style dialog box changes when you choose Style Contents

3 Click here, then choose required new options (or delete those you don't want by highlighting them and pressing [Delete]

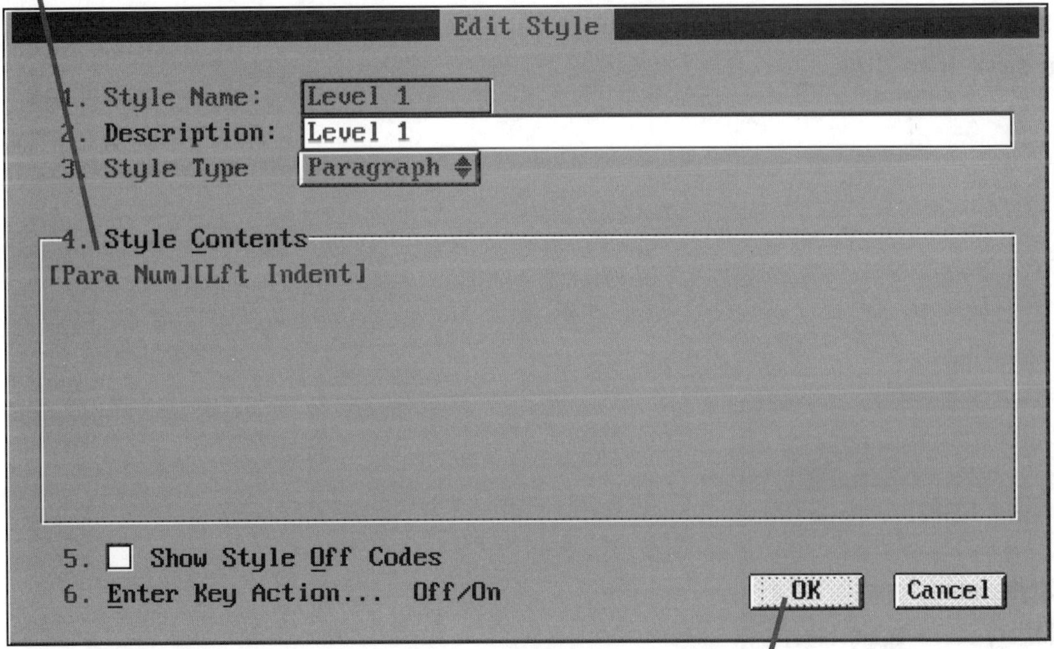

Edit Style
1. Style Name: Level 1
2. Description: Level 1
3. Style Type Paragraph
4. Style Contents
[Para Num][Lft Indent]
5. Show Style Off Codes
6. Enter Key Action... Off/On
OK
Cancel

Click to accept changes

Style libraries

WordPerfect lets you organise styles into collections known as *personal libraries.*

Style libraries are very useful. You can save styles which relate to a specific task into an appropriate library. For example, if you have styles which you normally use to produce a magazine, you could save them to a library known as *magazine.*

It's a good idea, incidentally, to allocate an unmistakable file extension to libraries for ease of recognition. WordPerfect Corporation recommends that you end library titles with the extension *.sty*. The magazine library would therefore be entitled: *magazine.sty*.

Once created, libraries (and their constituent styles) can be *retrieved* into other documents and are then immediately available. Styles which are retrieved in this way then become part of the new document when you save it to disk.

Basic steps:

SAVING STYLES INTO LIBRARIES

1. Choose **Layout↳Styles**, to call up the Style List dialog box (see page 132)
2. Click Save. This calls up the Save Styles dialog box
3. Enter a name for the library (WordPerfect automatically saves its library styles in your \WP60 directory)
4. Click OK

RETRIEVING LIBRARIES INTO DOCUMENTS

5. From within the relevant open document, follow Step 1 then click Retrieve. This calls up the Retrieve Styles dialog box
6. Enter the name of the library
7. Choose OK

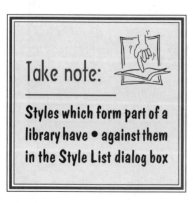

Take note:

Styles which form part of a library have • against them in the Style List dialog box

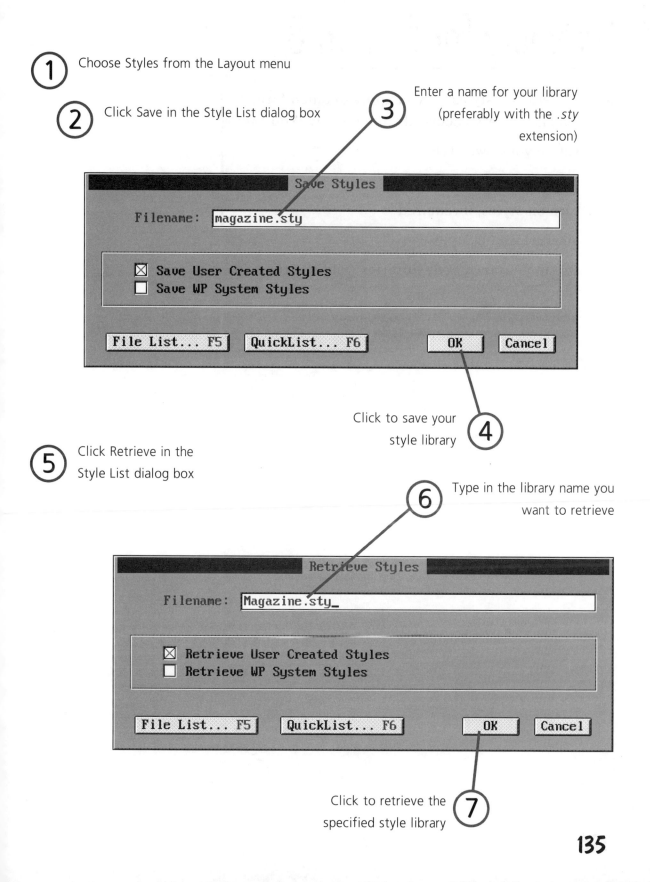

① Choose Styles from the Layout menu

② Click Save in the Style List dialog box

③ Enter a name for your library (preferably with the *.sty* extension)

Save Styles

Filename: magazine.sty

☒ Save User Created Styles
☐ Save WP System Styles

File List... F5   QuickList... F6   OK   Cancel

④ Click to save your style library

⑤ Click Retrieve in the Style List dialog box

⑥ Type in the library name you want to retrieve

Retrieve Styles

Filename: Magazine.sty_

☒ Retrieve User Created Styles
☐ Retrieve WP System Styles

File List... F5   QuickList... F6   OK   Cancel

⑦ Click to retrieve the specified style library

135

Summary for Section 8

● WordPerfect's styles let you apply detailed formatting commands very accurately and quickly. You can:

❏ set up your own styles

❏ apply styles to text

❏ turn off styles, if required

❏ amend existing styles

❏ set up your own style libraries (and use them in other documents).

9   Printing documents

Print Preview

Before you begin printing a document, it's a good idea to inspect it in Print Preview first.

WordPerfect's Graphics and Page modes provide an effective representation of what a document will look like when printed. Page mode is especially useful because it displays headers and footers as well as the main document text.

However, you should still use Print Preview to carry out a final proofing because it's more versatile. For instance, you can view successive pages at once as *thumbnails* for the rapid proofing of large documents.

If you have a mouse, you can access all of Print Preview's features by clicking on buttons in the overhead button bar.

What Print Preview displays depends on which WordPerfect printer driver is currently effective on your system. However, even if your printer isn't capable of printing graphics images in colour, they will still display accurately if you have a colour monitor.

Take note:

You can't edit documents from within Print Preview

1 Choose **File→Print Preview**. The display changes to Print Preview mode

2 Print Preview defaults to full page view. For a close up of the page, click the [Zoom In] button. Do this as often as necessary.

3 Click the [Zoom Out] button to see more of the page

4 Click the [FacngPgs] button to view two consecutive pages at once

5 To view thumbnail images, click the appropriate button [Thumb 8] or [Thumb 32]

6 To view the previous or subsequent pages, click the [PrevPage] or [NextPage] buttons

7 To jump to another page, click the [GotoPage] button

8 Enter the page number you want to go to and click OK

9 Press [F7] to return to your normal document window

138

(1) Choose Print Preview from the File menu

Click here to
zoom in (2)

Click here to
zoom out (3)

Click here to view
two pages (4)

Click here to jump
to another page (7)

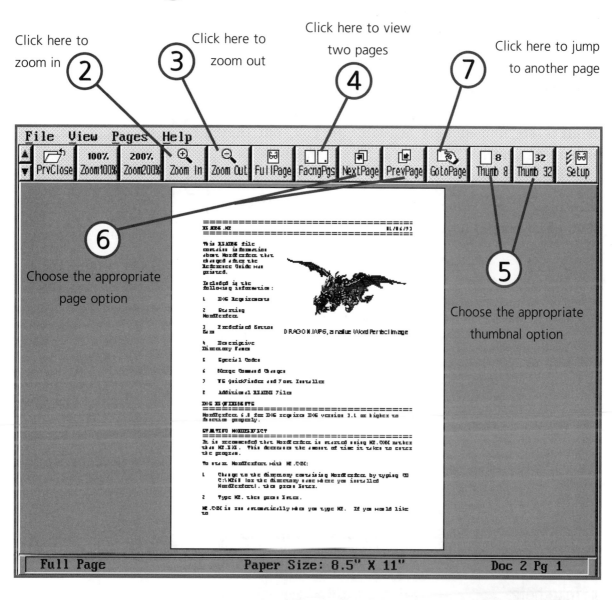

Choose the appropriate
page option

(6)

(5)

Choose the appropriate
thumbnal option

File   View   Pages   Help

PrvClose | Zoom100% | Zoom200% | Zoom In | Zoom Out | FullPage | FacngPgs | NextPage | PrevPage | GotoPage | Thumb 8 | Thumb 32 | Setup

Full Page   Paper Size: 8.5" X 11"   Doc 2 Pg 1

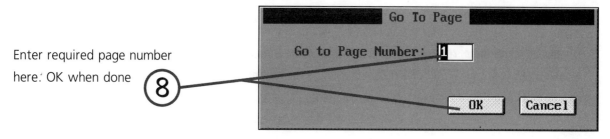

Enter required page number
here: OK when done (8)

Go To Page

Go to Page Number: 1

OK   Cancel

Selecting a printer

When you install WordPerfect 6, you normally opt to install at least one printer.

At the same time, WordPerfect also installs details of similar printers. These details are stored on your hard disk in one inclusive file whose suffix is *.all*. Any of these printers are immediately available to you, but they have to be *selected* before you can use them.

Some printers have more than one driver associated with them. For instance, the Hewlett Packard Deskjet 500C colour inkjet has:

● Black Pen

● Color Pen.

Normally, Black Pen would be selected. However, if you wanted to print in colour or in a combination of black and colour, you'd have to select Color Pen.

SELECTING A PRINTER DRIVER

1 Choose **File↦Print/Fax**. This calls up the Print/Fax dialog box

2 Click Select. This calls up the Select Printer dialog box

3 Double-click the correct printer (or highlight it and click Select)

Take note:

If you want to install a printer which wasn't included in your *.all* file during installation, re-run the installation program from the master disks (see your WordPerfect documentation for information on this) and follow the on-screen instructions

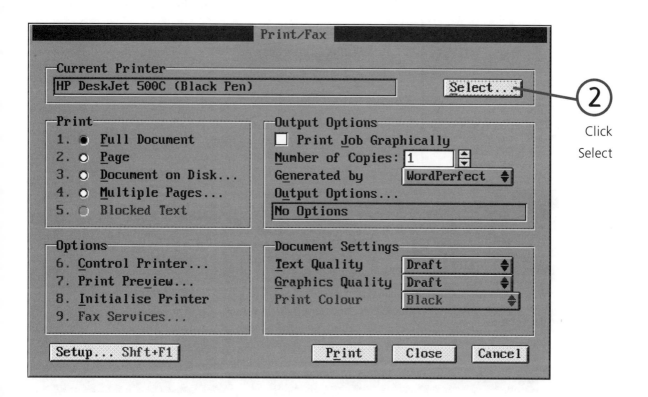

(1) Choose Print/Fax from the File menu

(2) Click Select

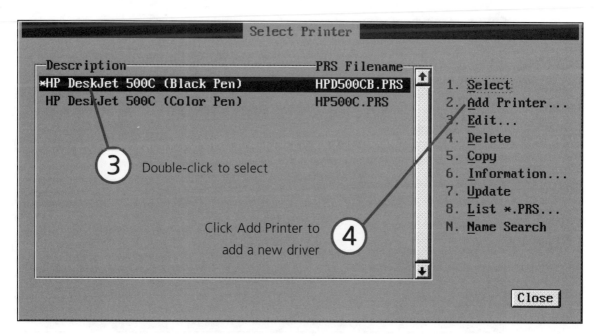

(3) Double-click to select

Click Add Printer to
add a new driver (4)

Selecting a printer (contd)

Basic steps:

ADDING NEW DRIVERS

4 Follow Steps 1–3. Select Add Printer. This calls up the Add Printers dialog box

5 Double-click the new printer (or highlight it and click Select)

6 In the Printer Filename dialog box, click OK. This calls up the Information dialog box

7 Click Close. This calls up the Edit Printer Setup dialog box

8 Click OK to confirm the default settings for the new printer

9 To use the new printer, back in the Select Printer dialog box, double-click it (or highlight it and click Select)

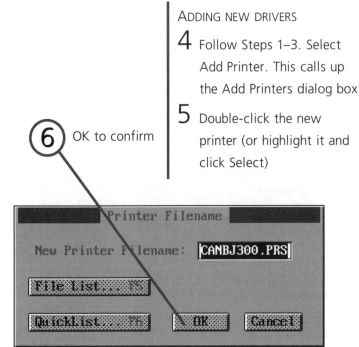

⑥ OK to confirm

Printer Filename

New Printer Filename: CANBJ300.PRS

File List...
QuickList   OK   Cancel

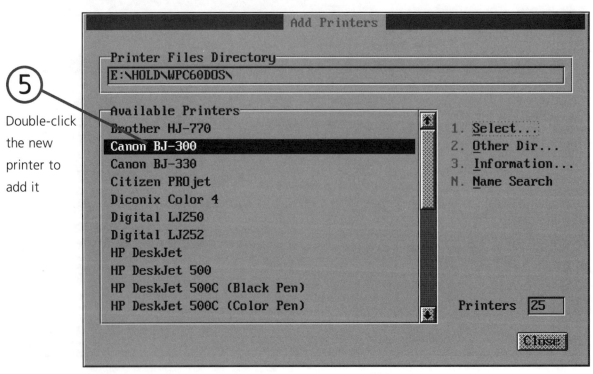

⑤ Double-click the new printer to add it

Add Printers

Printer Files Directory
E:\HOLD\WPC60DOS\

Available Printers
Brother HJ-770
Canon BJ-300
Canon BJ-330
Citizen PROjet
Diconix Color 4
Digital LJ250
Digital LJ252
HP DeskJet
HP DeskJet 500
HP DeskJet 500C (Black Pen)
HP DeskJet 500C (Color Pen)

1. Select...
2. Other Dir...
3. Information...
N. Name Search

Printers 25

Close

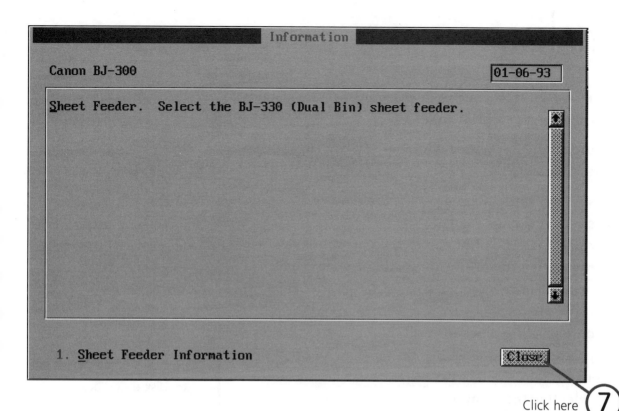

Information

Canon BJ-300   01-06-93

<u>S</u>heet Feeder. Select the BJ-330 (Dual Bin) sheet feeder.

1. <u>S</u>heet Feeder Information   Close

Click here ⑦

Edit Printer Setup

PRS Filename CANBJ300.PRS
Printer Name Canon BJ-300

1. <u>D</u>escription: Canon BJ-300

Hardware Options
2. ● <u>P</u>ort...   LPT1:
3. ○ <u>N</u>etwork Port...
4. <u>S</u>heet Feeder...   NO SHEET FEEDER DEFINED
5. ☐ Printer Configured for Colour

Fonts
6. <u>F</u>ont Setup...   Courier 10cpi
7. Directory for So<u>f</u>t Fonts:
   (and Printer Command Files)

Directory Tree... F8   QuickList F6   OK   Cancel

⑧ OK to confirm

143

Printing

Once a printer has been selected (see previous pages), WordPerfect can print to it.

You can choose from a wide variety of print options. These include:

- specifying the number of copies required
- specifying page ranges
- restricting the print run to the current page
- restricting the print run to odd or even pages
- printing in reverse page order (from the last to the first page)
- only printing blocked text
- printing from a disk file (rather than an open document)
- selecting the print quality.

Here are some examples of acceptable page ranges:

- 1-9 pages 1 to 9 inclusive
- 1,3,5-7,9,13 pages 1, 3, 5, 6, 7, 9 and 13
- 4- from page 4 to the end of the document
- -7 from page 1 as far as page 7.

Basic steps:

1 Choose **File→Print/Fax**. This calls up the Print/Fax dialog box

2 Click Page to print the current page

3 If you've blocked text prior to launching the Print/Fax dialog box, click Blocked Text to print it

4 To print a file on disk, click Document on Disk. This calls up the Document on Disk dialog box

5 Enter the name of the document you want to print

6 To specify print quality for text, click Text Quality. From the drop-down list select either Do Not Print, Draft, Medium or High

7 To specify the number of copies required, enter the correct number in the number box

① Choose Print/Fax from the File menu

Click here to print
the current page

④ Click here to call up the
Document on Disk dialog box

Enter number of copies
required ⑦

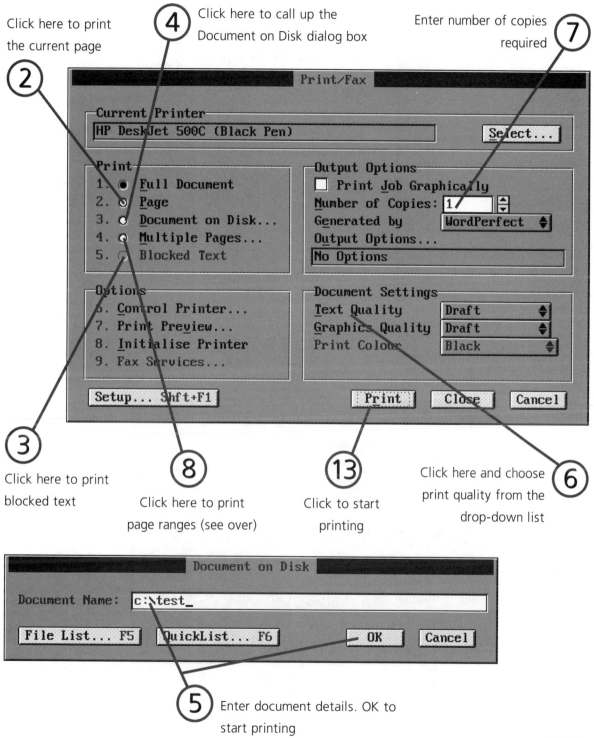

② ③

Click here to print
blocked text

⑧ Click here to print
page ranges (see over)

⑬ Click to start
printing

⑥ Click here and choose
print quality from the
drop-down list

⑤ Enter document details. OK to
start printing

Printing (contd)

8 To do any of the following:

❏ print page ranges
❏ print even or odd pages
❏ print in reverse order,

click on Multiple Pages,
which calls up the Print
Multiple Pages dialog box,
then follow Steps 10, 11 or
12 as appropriate

9 Enter the appropriate page
range in the Page/Label
Range field

10 Click Odd/Even Pages.
Select Odd or Even from
the drop–down list

11 Click Descending Order
(Last Page First)

12 Click OK, to return to
the Print/Fax dialog box

13 Click Print in the Print/
Fax dialog box to proceed
with the print job

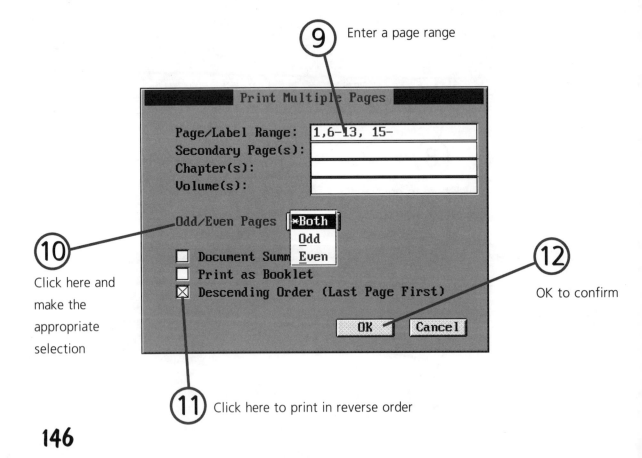

9 Enter a page range

Print Multiple Pages

Page/Label Range: 1,6–13, 15–
Secondary Page(s):
Chapter(s):
Volume(s):

Odd/Even Pages [*Both]
                  Odd
                  Even

10 Click here and make the appropriate selection

☐ Document Summ
☐ Print as Booklet
☒ Descending Order (Last Page First)

OK   Cancel

12 OK to confirm

11 Click here to print in reverse order

146

File Manager printing

You can use WordPerfect's File Manager (see Section 3 for further information on how to use this) as a convenient way to print documents stored on disk without having to use the Print/Fax dialog box (discussed on pages 144–146).

Basic steps:

1 Choose **File⤷File Manager**. In the Specify File Manager List dialog box, locate the directory you want and click OK to call up File Manager

2 Highlight the file you want to print and click Print. The Print Multiple Pages dialog box is called up. Follow steps 9–12 opposite

(2) Highlight the file you want to print, and select Print

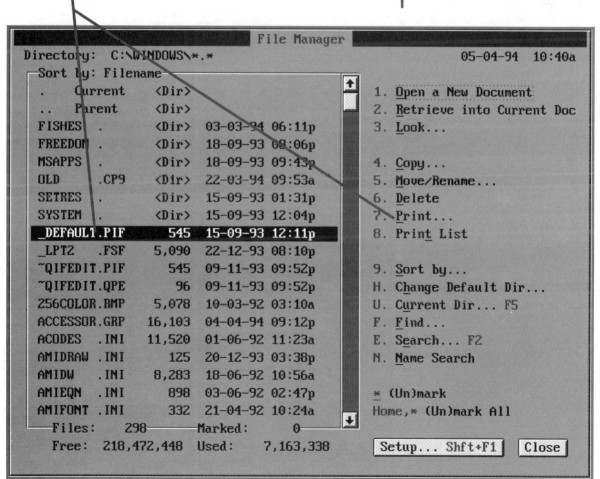

```
                                    File Manager
Directory:   C:\WINDOWS\*.*                          05-04-94   10:40a
 Sort by: Filename
 .      Current      <Dir>                    1.  Open a New Document
 ..     Parent       <Dir>                    2.  Retrieve into Current Doc
 FISHES  .           <Dir>  03-03-94 06:11p   3.  Look...
 FREEDOM .           <Dir>  18-09-93 08:06p
 MSAPPS  .           <Dir>  18-09-93 09:43p   4.  Copy...
 OLD     .CP9        <Dir>  22-03-94 09:53a   5.  Move/Rename...
 SETRES  .           <Dir>  15-09-93 01:31p   6.  Delete
 SYSTEM  .           <Dir>  15-09-93 12:04p   7.  Print...
 _DEFAUL1.PIF         545   15-09-93 12:11p   8.  Print List
 _LPT2   .FSF       5,090   22-12-93 08:10p
 ~QIFEDIT.PIF         545   09-11-93 09:52p   9.  Sort by...
 ~QIFEDIT.QPE          96   09-11-93 09:52p   H.  Change Default Dir...
 256COLOR.BMP       5,078   10-03-92 03:10a   U.  Current Dir... F5
 ACCESSOR.GRP      16,103   04-04-94 09:12p   F.  Find...
 ACODES  .INI      11,520   01-06-92 11:23a   E.  Search... F2
 AMIDRAW .INI         125   20-12-93 03:38p   N.  Name Search
 AMIDW   .INI       8,283   18-06-92 10:56a
 AMIEQN  .INI         898   03-06-92 02:47p   *  (Un)mark
 AMIFONT .INI         332   21-04-92 10:24a   Home,* (Un)mark All
  Files:    298        Marked:       0
  Free:  218,472,448  Used:   7,163,338    Setup... Shft+F1    Close
```

Summary for Section 9

● Printing is a WordPerfect 6.0 for DOS speciality (it supports far more printers than just about any other word processor).

● You can:

❑ proofread documents with complete precision in Print Preview

❑ use additional printers

❑ print documents with a host of options

❑ use File Manager to perform certain limited print actions.

Index